Old
Testament Books
for Pastor
and Teacher

Books by Brevard S. Childs
Published by The Westminster Press

Old Testament Books for Pastor and Teacher

The Book of Exodus, A Critical Theological Commentary
(Old Testament Library)

Biblical Theology in Crisis

Old Testament Books for Pastor and Teacher

by Brevard S. Childs

THE WESTMINSTER PRESS
Philadelphia

Published by The Westminster Press®
Philadelphia, Pennsylvania

PRINTED IN THE UNITED STATES OF AMERICA

Library of Congress Cataloging in Publication Data

Childs, Brevard S
 Old Testament books for pastor and teacher.

 Bibliography: p.
 Includes index.
 1. Bible. O.T.—Bibliography. I. Title.
 Z7772.A1C48 [BS1140.2]   016.2216   76–52457
 ISBN 0–664–24120–4

Contents

Preface   7

I.   Aim and Approach   9
II.   Theological Bibliographies   13
III. Basic Exegetical Tools   15
IV.   English Translations   17
V.   Biblical Dictionaries and Encyclopedias   19
VI.   Old Testament Introductions   22
VII. Biblical History and Background   24
VIII. Old Testament Theology   26
IX.   History of Exegesis   28
X.   Major Modern Commentaries Series   31
XI.   One-Volume Commentaries   33
XII. Individual Commentaries

1.	Genesis	35	13.	Esther	55
2.	Exodus	38	14.	Job	57
3.	Leviticus	41	15.	Psalms	59
4.	Numbers	42	16.	Proverbs	64
5.	Deuteronomy	42	17.	Ecclesiastes	66
6.	Joshua	44	18.	Song of Songs	68
7.	Judges	46	19.	Isaiah	70
8.	Ruth	48	20.	Jeremiah	74
9.	Samuel	49	21.	Lamentations	76
10.	Kings	50	22.	Ezekiel	77
11.	Chronicles	52	23.	Daniel	79
12.	Ezra, Nehemiah	54	24.	Minor Prophets	81

Abbreviations   89
Bibliography   91
Appendix   116
Index   117

Preface

The task of using the Bible faithfully and effectively in the ministry of the Christian church has always been a challenge for each new generation, but particularly within recent years the problem has increased in intensity. A widespread confusion has fallen upon large segments of the church regarding the nature of the Bible. This malaise has spread from clergy to laity, from old to young. How should the Bible be preached and taught? What should its role be in shaping the life of modern Christians? How does Scripture exert its authority on a congregation?

These problems are closely related to the larger theological crisis of our age in which older traditional positions have been abandoned and new ones have not yet been found. It is my conviction that the present struggle for a fresh theological formulation of the Christian faith will fail unless it is accompanied by a new understanding of the central place of the Bible within the church.

The attempt to turn over the study of the Bible to the professional scholar in the university and seminary has been of mixed blessing for the church. In spite of impressive advances in some areas of Biblical interpretation which modern scholarship has achieved, it remains a puzzlement why the general knowledge of Scripture continues to decline among both clergy and laity. Moreover, the basic theological task of using the Bible for instruction in the ways of God continues to be as obscure as ever for many.

I believe that it is of the highest priority for the church to seek to recover an understanding of its Scripture. This task cannot be accomplished by assigning it to a dispassionate battery of experts (although I do not doubt that God can work even in committees) but must arise from within the confessing church itself. This goal will not be reached without much prayer, struggle, and study of Scripture on the local parish level. Only seldom has rebirth begun in the academy. Of course, there is an important role for trained scholars, but their contribution must remain in the context of the worshiping community if it would address the pressing theological needs of the church.

This book grows out of a concern to reverse the trend of alienation and ignorance toward the Bible within the church. It is offered as a modest first step in aiding the pastor and the teacher in the use of the Old Testament for the Christian ministry. It seeks to address the practical issues of describing the resources at hand, and in building a working library at a reasonable cost. If these suggestions will at least begin to engage pastors critically with the church's rich exegetical heritage in the light of today's challenge, the book will have been well worth the effort.

B.S.C.

Yale University
New Haven, Connecticut

I

Aim and Approach

The purpose of this book is to provide a guide to the literature of the Old Testament as a resource for the ministry of the Christian church. The discussion is directed primarily to the pastor engaged in the serious study of Scripture. However, because the task of the preaching ministry is closely akin to that of the teaching ministry, I have sought to address the scholar of the church along with the pastor. I see no qualitative difference in their both sharing in the Christian ministry as a learned profession. Particularly at a time in which the image of the minister has been severely eroded by much confusion, it seems important to seek to recover the role of the pastor as both the spiritual and the intellectual leader of the flock.

The book list has a very practical aim in mind. It seeks to aid the pastor in the purchase and use of books, and to make suggestions on how best to build a working Old Testament library as a resource for ministry. To achieve this goal it is essential that critical evaluations be made of the available literature in an effort to determine levels of excellence, richness in content, and priority of choice. Obviously the issue of the criteria on which such judgments rest must be immediately faced.

By offering to the minister a practical guide to the books in the field of Old Testament I am also attempting to make an assessment of the discipline from a theological perspective. At the outset it should be clearly stated that I am approaching the field of Old Testament from the stance of one who seeks to understand its role as Scripture of the church. The criteria of evaluation arise from within this context of faith. This move does not imply that this context is the only legitimate one from which to study the Old Testament. Obviously within our modern pluralistic society the options are numerous. However, I would argue strongly for the integrity of this confessional stance. My criteria for evaluating the literature derive from its usefulness in the task of rendering the text as Scripture of the church. By fixing the discussion within the context of the church's use of Scripture I am not seeking to arrive at criteria of evaluation in terms of one given doctrinal position. There has always been a wide range of differing opinions within the church's tradition which should be respected and maintained. But it does suggest that a commitment to the Bible as canonical Scripture does imply some significant corollaries that have been shared by all the branches of the Christian church.

Thus, it is a broad Christian conviction that God has always faithfully addressed the church through the medium of Scripture and promises to do so in the future. Again, it is believed that the Bible contains the truthful witness to the prophetic and apostolic tradition, and that the role of the Spirit of God ensures the message of the Bible from being anchored in the historical past. Finally, the Bible addresses a living word of judgment and redemption to the church and the world in each successive generation.

In the history of the Christian church different ways have been used to express the theological understanding of the normative role of Scripture in the life of the church. Some theologians have spoken of the "presence of God in Scripture," others of "hearing the Word of God," or of having the tradition of the past "made alive" for the present through God's Spirit. In spite of these differences in formulation, a particular attitude toward the church's special relationship to the Bible has distinguished it from a variety of other nonconfessional approaches. One of the criteria of a book's usefulness to the pastor turns on the contribution of an author to this dimension of Scripture's role within the church.

It is obvious that the church's use of Scripture has varied greatly over the centuries. One only has to contrast the approach of the church fathers, the Reformers, and the post-Enlightenment Christians to see the enormous variety. Yet the commitment to the Bible as a living vehicle through which God instructs the church has been a consistent quality of Christian interpretation, even when poorly executed.

The rise of the historical critical method in the middle of the eighteenth century, culminating in its complete hegemony by the end of the nineteenth century, brought an enormous new set of resources as well as a nest of disturbing new questions regarding the church's understanding of the Bible. For well over one hundred and fifty years theologians have wrestled with the issue of relating the new critical methodologies to the Christian faith. It is not my purpose to rehearse the theological debate at this juncture, but, in my opinion, the basic theological problems remain far from being resolved. Frequently a sterile impasse has emerged between the conservative and the liberal elements within the church. In my evaluation of books, I am critical of a conservative stance that rejects the insights of literary criticism from the outset on dogmatic grounds and seeks to return to the past. Conversely, I am equally dissatisfied with the reigning liberal stance that assumes the normative role of historical criticism in determining the Bible's meaning and shows little understanding of the theological issues at stake for the life of the church. The frequently suggested compromise that our commentaries need only supply a theological topping to sweeten the hard crust of historical critical exegesis simply does not come to grips with the issue.

I do not believe that this complex theological problem will be solved by a new and cleverer theological proposal. The level of understanding that is being sought requires a profounder wrestling with Scripture by a broad segment of the church as part of its life of praise and service. This book list is offered as a modest aid in this search for a renewed understanding of the Bible by the Christian community.

The bibliographical suggestions are not intended to reflect a consensus, but are my own personal evaluations. However, I trust that they will not appear idiosyncratic but will stand solidly within the mainstream of historic Christianity. Although I have made no claim to be exhaustive, I hope that the selection is representative of the resources available. My concern is not to inculcate a narrow doctrinal position, but rather to determine elements of excellence among the various books and relate these contributions to the church's exegetical task. I am fully convinced that good and bad exegesis cuts across doctrinal lines and is represented at both ends of the theological spectrum. A variety in quality is also found in all periods of the church's history, which observation contradicts the widespread opinion that the latest commentary is necessarily the best.

I also apply a negative criterion to books that appear ignorant of the data, are slovenly in execution, and are lacking in thoroughness, regardless of how pious. I shall be critical of commentators who are idiosyncratic and overly speculative. I shall seek to apprise the reader of dogmatic categories—whether liberal or conservative is irrelevant—which block a close hearing of the text. Finally, I shall try to judge the level of penetration and the degree of genuine exegetical insightfulness.

This book list is not intended to remove the need for the pastor's critical discernment in the use of the resources. Regardless of the excellence of a book, whether by Augustine or Bultmann, my commendation assumes a careful and critical scrutiny on the part of the modern reader. No one can eliminate a degree of subjectivity in judgment, and some books that are highly recommended here will probably offer no help to some.

I have also tried to be sensitive to the variety of functions that are performed by different authors and their books. Some volumes have an important place because of their quantity of useful information. Other volumes excel in lucid popularization of complex issues. And others serve to stimulate and provide invaluable aid to the homiletical needs of the preacher. I am also aware that a pastor reflects different moods and often needs a change from heavy commentaries to poetic paraphrase.

At times I make mention of books that are not easily accessible or that are written in French or German. These suggestions can be ignored by the average pastor, but they are included for the sake of completeness and as a challenge to the continuing education of the church's leaders. To underestimate the intellectual capacity of the clergy is a far more grievous fault than to set the standard too high.

II

Theological
Bibliographies

The suggestions that now follow are not intended to duplicate the several excellent bibliographical manuals directed to Biblical research. Rather, I shall focus on certain volumes that I have found most useful in learning about the literature available and in assessing its quality. I particularly prize a closely annotated bibliography.

The two standard modern manuals, by Frederick W. Danker and by George S. Glanzman, offer reliable and accurate guides into the material. Particularly Danker's rich discussion of all the tools for Bible study is excellent and highly recommended. My main criticism is that the discussion fails to deal adequately with the older literature and does not offer the needed advice in evaluating the various books. In my opinion, Danker's suggested list of commentaries leaves much to be desired. Another highly useful modern tool is the annual *Book List* published by the British Society for Old Testament Study. These lists offer a brief, critical review of almost everything that appears in the field, often indicating its practical value for the pastor or the teacher. The lists from 1946 through 1973 have been reprinted in three volumes and are available in any good seminary library. The volumes have been edited by H. H. Rowley, George W. Anderson, and Peter R. Ackroyd.

I would also mention a number of bibliographies on theological literature that treat the older literature in detail. James Darling's *Cyclopaedia* is an invaluable resource on the whole range of theological literature. In the first volume there is a list of authors and their writings, with a brief biography. In the second volume exegetical studies and sermons from all periods of history are cataloged according to chapter and verse throughout the entire Bible. Thus at one's fingertips is important information on how a particular passage, such as the Decalogue, was interpreted in the history of exegesis.

I have found the *Introduction* of Alfred Cave most complete for English works in the last part of the nineteenth century, but for the earlier period, particularly for commentaries of the sixteenth century through the end of the eighteenth century, Thomas H. Horne's exhaustive list in Volume V of his *Introduction* has never been supplanted. This volume is frequently available cheaply on the secondhand-book market and should not be overlooked. William Orme's annotated list is also very useful for the same period. In addition, I consider Charles H. Spurgeon's *Commenting and Commentaries* a real classic. Obviously Spurgeon evaluated the literature from a rather rigid doctrinal stance, but he also had much skill and common sense in discerning the enduring qualities of excellence. His list has been reprinted.

Many theological schools have issued recommended lists of books and I have nearly a dozen of these lists. By and large, the lack of careful annotation lessens the value of these bibliographies, but even such attempts are better than nothing. I am unhappy with Cyril J. Barber's recently published volume, *The Minister's Library*, because I think his advice is very misleading. Barber seems mainly concerned with the orthodoxy of the author and he has little judgment of quality. The difference between Spurgeon and Barber in this respect could hardly be more striking. Also Wilbur M. Smith's conservative theological position has not beclouded his critical discernment.

Finally, for the sake of completeness, I would recommend the bibliographies of Georg B. Winer and Ernst A. Zuchold for the scholar working in German, and Jacob Le Long and Johann G. Walch for the Latin sources in the study of the Bible. Augustin Calmet is excellent for both early French and Latin.

III

Basic

Exegetical Tools

Once again, for a thorough discussion I would refer the student of Old Testament to Frederick Danker's work. My aim here, however, is to offer a few practical suggestions to the pastor on securing the basic tools.

Obviously one should have a critical edition of the Hebrew text, and at present Rudolf Kittel's *Biblia Hebraica* is about the only option. From a scholarly perspective the approach of Kittel to text criticism has been much criticized. There are far too many conjectures in his notes and the use of the versions is unreliable. Be that as it may, I would advise the pastor and the student also to learn to use an edition of the Hebrew Bible without elaborate footnotes, such as Norman H. Snaith's. By using only Kittel one is likely to gain the erroneous impression that the study of the Old Testament is akin to working with a mutilated crossword puzzle rather than reading a piece of literature. I think it is significant that most Jewish scholars who have a fluency in Hebrew avoid using Kittel. I would even suggest purchasing a pocket-sized Hebrew Bible from Israel and seeking to read at least the prose material at sight.

The Greek Old Testament, often referred to as the Septuagint, is an invaluable exegetical tool, not least because of its major role in the New Testament. Danker offers a discussion of the critical Cambridge and Göttingen editions, but for the working pastor I would suggest the very useful Henry B. Swete edition, which is often available secondhand. I certainly prefer it to

15

the eclectic text of Alfred Rahlfs. Also I would not disdain the old Samuel Bagster & Sons Greek and English edition as providing a very useful tool for the pastor whose Greek has grown rusty.

Usually a pastor's needs for a Hebrew grammar will be met by the elementary textbook from which he learned the language, but a few suggestions are in order for more advanced work. Thomas O. Lambdin's grammar has become widely used as a first-year grammar, and the quality is excellent. However, I find that Lambdin offers too much information for the first year and not really enough for advanced work. I would therefore still suggest the old Gesenius *Hebrew Grammar,* edited by Arthur E. Cowley, for advanced work. The many indexes make the volume a superb reference work that has not been superseded.

Certainly a good Hebrew lexicon is a desideratum for serious exegetical work. The edition edited by Francis Brown, Samuel R. Driver, and Charles A. Briggs is still the most thorough in English and far more reliable than the first edition of Ludwig Koehler and Walter Baumgartner. There is a shortened version of Koehler-Baumgartner by William L. Holladay which is useful, but it is rather expensive for its size. I would encourage the pastor to pick up cheaply one of the older nineteenth-century English translations of Gesenius—I prefer Edward Robinson to Samuel P. Tregelles—which are still serviceable if used with discretion.

There are several good Hebrew concordances, especially the inexpensive Israeli reprint of Solomon Mandelkern, but I would be more concerned that the pastor possess an adequate English concordance. The concordance to the Revised Standard Version edited by John W. Ellison has not replaced the more thorough older concordances to the Authorized Version. I would advise the pastor to secure either the concordance by Robert Young or by James Strong, particularly since these volumes are easy to secure rather cheaply on the used-book market. I would also not reject owning a Cruden's, especially if I inherited it from a parishioner.

IV

English

Translations

To offer an evaluation of the strengths and weaknesses of all the various English translations available is to raise a highly controversial issue. My major advice is that you acquaint yourself with several and use them in different situations. Obviously the *King James Version* will retain its unique place because of its excellence of language. It is hard to imagine memorizing a psalm in another translation. In recent years the *American Revised Version* of 1901 has lost some of its popularity, but it remains the most literal rendering of the Hebrew. *An American Translation,* often referred to as the Chicago Bible, was executed by several different scholars. The sections by Theophile J. Meek are the best and demonstrate a mastery of Hebrew syntax which is still without equal. The strengths of the *Revised Standard Version* are evident in its enormous popularity. It has been a success in offering a skillful compromise between the traditional and the modern.

I would also recommend the use of *The New English Bible* for its crisp new English style. Its rendering of much of the narrative material is quite brilliant and often casts a fresh light on an old passage. Unfortunately this translation suffers from idiosyncratic readings which have often arisen from speculation on the original pointing of the Hebrew. In questions of detail, the wise reader will remain cautious. It is to be hoped that these oddities will be removed in a subsequent edition and its true value emerge unimpaired. *The New American Bible* is a carefully done Catholic version comparable to the *Revised Standard Version,* but less brilliant than *The Jerusalem Bible.* The translation of the entire Old Testament by the Jewish Publication Society is in progress. The portions that have already appeared give evidence of a very mature, skillful job of translating.

I would also recommend the use of several of the more loosely paraphrased translations, such as *Today's English Version.* Often these new paraphrases actualize a text for a particular purpose, such as evangelism. A danger arises only when one forgets that such paraphrases are derivative and must be constantly measured by the full range of meaning and ambiguities which are supported by the canonical text.

In order to appreciate the theological significance of translating the Bible into the vernacular, I heartily recommend Martin Luther's brilliant essay "On Translating: An Open Letter," in Vol. 35 of *Luther's Works* (American Edition).

V

Biblical Dictionaries

and Encyclopedias

Danker's chapter on Bible dictionaries is unusually thorough and need not be repeated. Many different sorts of dictionaries are available which vary greatly in range of information, length of articles, and theological perspective. A pastor should have a clear understanding of what type of information he or she is acquiring when making a sizable investment in such a reference work.

I have never prized one-volume dictionaries of the Bible highly because the limited space permits only very brief paragraphs. Yet one could argue that speed and ease in acquiring information justifies such a volume. If so, the dictionaries of Henry Snyder Gehman and Madeleine S. and John L. Miller are options. Personally, I feel that the money could be better spent on a larger set.

Probably the most serviceable modern dictionary is *The Interpreter's Dictionary of the Bible,* edited by George A. Buttrick. A Supplementary Volume has recently appeared which brings the articles up to date. Although the articles are of mixed quality, generally a modern critical consensus is reflected. Much of the confusion within the discipline in regard to methodology is also evident, yet there are also some outstanding articles.

I find myself frequently supplementing the information of a modern critical dictionary with one of the older, so-called pre-critical sets. Mainly this move is caused by the loss of much important information that has been removed or forgotten in the newer approaches. A set that I prize highly is William Smith's *Dictionary of the Bible,* edited by Horatio B. Hackett. Not only are there superb articles on such subjects as "canon," "tabernacle," and "Bible," but each article is concluded with an elaborate bibliography of the history of exegesis. I also recommend John Kitto's *Cyclopaedia,* particularly in the third edition of William L. Alexander, for a learned presentation of the more traditional views regarding the canonical role of the various Biblical books. The third edition includes biographies on most of the important Biblical scholars.

Mention should also be made of the two large Bible dictionaries that were published in the period just before World War I, one edited by James Hastings and the other by Thomas K. Cheyne and John S. Black. Especially Hastings' dictionary is a monument of enormous learning. Generally the articles reflect the literary critical methods of the late nineteenth century and therefore have not held up too well. Still some articles in both sets are unsurpassed. These dictionaries are worth owning, if purchased cheaply and used critically. Less useful is the Bible dictionary edited by James Orr, which is apologetic and polemical.

Most of the larger English encyclopedias on religion are old and out-of-date, providing little help in the study of the Bible. I do not doubt that the research scholar can still find some value in James Hastings' famous *Encyclopaedia of Religion and Ethics,* but in my experience, the tendentious and heavy-handed use of comparative religion has blurred most of the Biblical material into an unusable shape. However, I have a different opinion of the encyclopedia edited by John McClintock and James Strong. Often I have found that the articles directly relating to Biblical exegesis lack the originality and thoroughness of William Smith's *Dictionary,* but there is a broad range of excellent articles on other subjects touching on the Bible, particularly the history of the discipline, which are unsurpassed.

Finally a word is in order regarding Gerhard Kittel's famous *Theological Dictionary of the New Testament.* No one doubts the enormous quantity of information incorporated in these volumes, much of which touches on the Old Testament. Personally, I find that I do not use the volumes as much as I once thought I would. I sense that there is a growing consensus that the isolation of particular words, regardless of how learned, is not the best way to approach Biblical exegesis, and that there is something artificial about Kittel's approach. In spite of its usefulness in understanding certain words and Biblical concepts, this enterprise initiated by Kittel as a means of recovering the theological dimension of the Bible cannot be deemed a success. I remain, therefore, undecided whether a pastor should invest this much money in the one set. At least I would urge trying out the library's copy before deciding. I have a similar opinion regarding the more recent *Theological Dictionary of the Old Testament,* edited by G. Johannes Botterweck and Helmer Ringgren.

The other larger wordbook, edited by Johannes B. Bauer, has had a somewhat mixed reception by its reviewers and is generally not in the same class with Kittel. However, for the special problems of Catholic theology and the Bible the volume is quite valuable. Two much more modest volumes can be recommended to provide a brief treatment of some key words; one is edited by Alan Richardson, the other by Jean Jacques von Allmen.

VI

Old Testament Introductions

The kind of information provided by an Old Testament Introduction is found in most good Bible dictionaries. Special volumes are hardly needed in a pastor's library. Usually the pastor has retained a seminary textbook in the field. The standard critical Introductions are those by Otto Eissfeldt, Georg Fohrer, and Otto Kaiser. I am far from satisfied with the picture that emerges of the Old Testament from these volumes, but I do not have a good alternative to suggest at the present time. The conservative Introductions by Merrill F. Unger, Roland K. Harrison, Gleason L. Archer, and Edward J. Young are mainly reactions to the critical approach, often highly polemical and tendentious, and they offer no fresh or creative alternative. In my opinion, neither the Introductions of the left nor of the right provide much exegetical aid in understanding the canonical text.

In the wake of the Biblical Theology Movement of the 1950's a more popular type of Introduction appeared which sought to combine the introductory questions of composition with a more interpretative, theological style. Among the more successful efforts could be listed the books of Bernhard W. Anderson and Norman K. Gottwald. These volumes still have some value, but tend to cover up the hard hermeneutical questions.

A far more creative effort to deal with the critical dimension of the formation of the Bible has been offered in the Fortress Press series *Guides to Biblical Scholarship,* edited by Gene M.

Tucker. Half a dozen lucid, informative brief paperbacks have appeared on the issues of form criticism, tradition criticism, and literary criticism. The most recent contributions on problems of text and history are of high caliber and are certainly to be highly recommended.

VII

Biblical History
and Background

Once again, this type of material is usually provided by a good Bible dictionary and does not call for duplication within a library. However, there are many useful and informative volumes that greatly enrich the Biblical background.

Among the modern histories of Israel available, John Bright's still has the edge over Martin Noth's for a lucid and thorough presentation. Both volumes are not without some measure of special pleading and should be used critically. The most recent history, by Siegfried Herrmann, is much oriented to the debate within Germany and is no substitute for either Bright or Noth.

Several good geographies of the Bible and atlases are available, and certainly a good library should have at least one. My preference would be either Herbert G. May's *Oxford Bible Atlas,* now in a paperback edition, or George Ernest Wright and Floyd V. Filson's *The Westminster Historical Atlas to the Bible.* The latter is getting somewhat old, but is of lasting quality. There is a competent historical geography by Yohanan Aharoni, which, however, lacks the brilliance and verve of George Adam Smith's classic volume.

For archaeological background, George Ernest Wright's *Biblical Archaeology* is probably still the best survey, but his perspective no longer carries a broad consensus as it once did in America. I would also recommend purchasing William F. Albright, *The Archaeology of Palestine,* as a splendid paperback bargain, and the impressive volume edited by David Winton Thomas, *Archaeology and Old Testament Study,* for a series of excellent survey articles.

A fascinating collection of articles has also appeared in the three paperback volumes of the *Biblical Archaeologist Reader.* Finally, the well-known book of Roland de Vaux, *Ancient Israel,* deserves high commendation for bringing the various historical disciplines to bear on a remarkable study of Israel's institutions, including such basic subjects as family, law, and cult.

VIII

Old Testament
Theology

Two major theologies of the Old Testament have dominated the field for the last thirty years. Walther Eichrodt's magisterial set, which was written in the period just before World War II, excels in its comprehensive survey of the thought world of the Old Testament set over against the culture of the Ancient Near East. Gerhard von Rad's brilliant reformulation of the discipline along the lines of the history of traditions has been a seminal work for twenty years in a measure equaled only by Rudolf Bultmann's *Theology of the New Testament.* It is hard to believe that a serious pastor could not profit from a close study of these two sets. Needless to say, both theologies rest on a particular method of research which needs to be constantly checked with the canonical text itself. In my opinion, the several other modern Old Testament theologies of Theodorus C. Vriezen, Edmond Jacob, and John L. McKenzie have been eclipsed by the two giants in the field. However, I would recommend James Barr's book *Old and New in Interpretation* for an incisive criticism of the field of Biblical theology.

Quite often one can find several of the older nineteenth-century theologies of the Old Testament on the secondhand-book market. Much of the material has lost its value because of the dominant philosophical categories that were used to order Biblical material. Nevertheless, there is some useful

26

handling of important topics which the contemporary theologies have sorely neglected. I prefer Andrew B. Davidson's theology to that of either Gustav F. Oehler or Hermann Schultz, but all are worth buying, if procured inexpensively.

IX

History of Exegesis

One of the greatest liabilities arising from the hegemony of the historical critical method has been to sever sharply the history of the church's exegetical traditions with the past. The impression is given that little of any value in respect to serious study of the Bible preceded the rise of nineteenth-century critical insight. In my opinion, this widespread sentiment represents a disastrous misunderstanding of the role of Scripture within the life of the church. There is an enormous need to recover the richness of the church's exegetical traditions. The task requires skill, learning, and devout struggle and I urge the serious pastor to strive to recover his theological heritage.

Since the standard critical Introductions are the greatest offenders in blocking all avenues to the past, I would recommend other volumes as aids. *The Cambridge History of the Bible,* edited by Stanley L. Greenslade, is unfortunately of very mixed quality, but still offers important insights into the various periods and has full bibliographies. The set is available in a paperback edition and is of excellent value. Beryl Smalley's *The Study of the Bible in the Middle Ages* is a magnificent volume which is also available in paperback. She offers a brilliant insight into the excitement and depth of medieval interpretation. For the period of the Reformation, I would suggest Heinrich Bornkamm and James S. Preus for the study of Luther, and Thomas H. L. Parker and Hans Heinrich Wolf for Calvin. One of my favorite books for this period is Arnold Williams' *The Common Expositor,* which includes the best of Catholic interpretation along with the Reformers. Perhaps the finest introduction to the issues of so-called pre-critical exegesis is offered by Hans Frei in his brilliant study of eighteenth-century hermeneutics. Although many other volumes touch on the history of exegesis, such as the introductory articles in the *Jerome Biblical Commentary,* most of them evaluate the contributions of the past in proportion to their success in adumbrating the later critical exegesis. It is exactly this misunderstanding which must be overcome if any real recovery is to be made.

I am well aware of the difficulties facing a modern reader who begins to work in the exegesis of the church fathers. For this reason I would advise the student to begin with the Reformation period and slowly work back. The study of the church fathers is made more difficult because much of the best in the exegesis has never been translated into English, particularly in the area of Old Testament. Indeed there are some classic treatments available such as Augustine on the Psalter and Gregory on Job, but neither provides an easy access. I would rather suggest reading sections in Augustine's *City of God* that relate to the Old Testament as an introduction and only then return to the Psalter. Unfortunately, only Chrysostom's commentaries on the New Testament are translated, as is also the case with Theodore. Jerome's commentary on Daniel is available in English, but his lovely commentary on Jonah is still only in French. Origen on the Song of Songs would only confirm the suspicion of most Protestants against the church fathers.

When we turn to the Reformation period, again one is faced with the problem of translations. Most of the great corpus of Reformation exegesis by Huldreich Zwingli, Johann Brenz, Martin Bucer, Philip Melanchthon, Peter Martyr Vermigli, and others is still buried in Latin. Fortunately, this is not the case with either Luther or Calvin. I would heartily recommend to the pastor to read deeply and widely in these two great Biblical interpreters. Perhaps it is wise to start with Calvin, whose commentaries have appeared in paperback editions, but Luther's robust and profound commentaries offer an inexhaustible resource for the proclamation of the gospel.

Much of the great exegesis of the seventeenth century is also buried in such collections as the *Critici Sacri,* edited by John Pearson, and the *Synopsis Criticorum,* edited by Matthew Poole.

Ernst F. K. Rosenmüller's multivolumed set of *Scholia* is very useful for the history of exegesis in the eighteenth century, but is also in Latin. At least the great Catholic expositor, Augustin Calmet, is available in French. I would strongly recommend that pastors secure one of the great English pastors who wrote commentaries on the whole Bible—namely, Matthew Henry, Thomas Scott, and Adam Clarke. One should not settle for an abbreviated modern edition, but should purchase the unabridged edition on the secondhand-book market. Needless to say, the modern reader must exercise skill and acute discernment in using these volumes. These old books can work as a trap and deception if the pastor is simply looking for a retreat into the past, but if they are correctly used, innumerable riches can be tapped. The same judgment holds true for many of the old Puritan commentaries which are being reprinted.

A very valuable guide into the history of exegesis is provided by Wilfrid Werbeck. He has listed the major commentators on each Biblical book throughout the history of the church in an appendix to the individual articles in the third edition of *Die Religion in Geschichte und Gegenwart,* edited by Kurt Galling.

X

Major Modern Commentaries Series

It is common knowledge that the quality of individual commentaries varies greatly within any given series. Usually one can expect a few excellent volumes, many mediocre, and a few quite poor ones. For this reason, it is a rule of thumb for a pastor never to buy a whole series, but to seek to determine the best volumes in a series. Danker's chapter on the major series is thorough and need not be duplicated. However, a few words to characterize the various series are in order.

The *International Critical Commentary* is the most technical series available in English which covers most of the Old Testament. For a certain type of technical work, especially on text and history, the material contained has never been surpassed in its thoroughness. However, most of the volumes are out-of-date and without serious theological interest. The average pastor and teacher will find the *Old Testament Library* to be a more useful resource for their needs. It is semipopular in character. A very high level of technical scholarship is evidenced in the new series *Hermeneia,* but too few volumes have appeared in the Old Testament to make a prediction on its total value.

The reader will see that in my detailed discussion of individual commentaries I make much reference to some of the old, more popular series. Several excellent volumes appeared in the old *Expositor's Bible* and in the *Cambridge Bible.* Somewhat fewer of really first-rate quality were published in the *Century Bible* and the *Westminster,* but these were outstanding. Of this older period, the series by Carl F. Keil and by Franz Delitzsch, even though they are very conservative in orientation—this is especially true of Keil—can be relied upon for a consistently serious handling of the text. In the form of an inexpensive reprint, these two authors remain excellent buys.

I am far from enthusiastic about the well-known *Interpreter's Bible.* I think the division between exegesis and exposition was a fundamental error and destroys the inner dynamic of serious theological reflection. The homiletical observations strike me as usually thin and moralistic. In this regard, the *Broadman's Bible* is an improvement. But the general level is too low really to satisfy. The attempt to compromise between a modern historical critical approach and a traditional, conservative Protestant free church theology has not been successful. Little of the critical work is fresh or creative, whereas the theology lacks the robust quality and sharp cutting edge that one has learned to expect from evangelical Protestantism. I am afraid that the series has fallen between two stools.

Several of *The Anchor Bible* commentaries receive high commendation. The chief strength lies in the excellent new translations. Some are quite unusable. It now appears that the writers are allowed great freedom in the format and it is therefore dangerous to generalize regarding future volumes. Even though the price has remained quite reasonable for the size of the books, one should choose carefully. Fortunately, several of the authors have broken away from the original concept of a narrow philological and historical orientation.

Finally, mention should be made of the several very popular, even elementary series of commentaries. Although the level is really too elementary to be used by most pastors, the *New Cambridge Bible* does have a value for use by Sunday school teachers and lay persons. At times I feel that the theological level is quite thin, but much of modern critical research is attractively presented to the beginner. I am less enthusiastic about the *New Century Bible,* which is a semipopular approach without anything unique or striking. In the detailed comments that follow on individual books I have also evaluated commentaries in the *Torch Bible, Layman's Bible Commentary,* and *Tyndale Old Testament Commentaries.*

XI

One-Volume

Commentaries

One-volume commentaries provide easy access to basic information about the Bible in a brief and summary fashion. The disadvantage is that one can hardly expect great depth of insight or a thorough handling of the subject. Within these limitations two sets stand preeminent. *The Jerome Biblical Commentary,* edited by Raymond E. Brown and others, contains a highly impressive set of introductory articles on the Bible which cover the widest range possible. A detailed bibliography precedes each article. Such topics as "Introduction to Wisdom Literature," "Modern Old Testament Criticism," "Biblical Geography," and "Hermeneutics" are of high quality and packed with pertinent information. I am somewhat less impressed with the actual exegesis of each book, where the lack of real penetration is often all too evident. Nevertheless, the volume is impressive and belongs in every good church library.

Peake's Commentary on the Bible, edited by Matthew Black and H. H. Rowley, is also of high quality within the given limitations imposed on a one-volume commentary. Many of the great names are represented and there is a strong emphasis on archaeology. Several of the articles have become classics, such as Robert B. Y. Scott on "weights and measures." The scope of the articles is not as wide or massive as in *The Jerome Biblical Commentary,* but I would give Peake the clear edge when it comes to exegesis. For example, James Barr's handling of Daniel is creative and fresh.

Two other modern one-volume commentaries are available

—one is edited by Charles M. Laymon, the other by Donald Guthrie—but I do not evaluate them as highly. The older sets, such as the commentary by Charles Gore and the 1920 edition of Arthur S. Peake, are quite dated, but they have retained some value and should not be disposed of, if inherited.

XII

Individual

Commentaries

1. Genesis

Because of the obvious importance of the Book of Genesis for the entire Bible, one is not surprised to find an enormous amount of exegetical literature on Genesis. Serious commentaries and lengthy treatises on the book extend from the earliest period to the modern era with unbroken regularity. Although there are many excellent commentaries from which to choose, some of the most useful exegetical work appears in other forms than that of the commentary and should not be overlooked.

In my judgment, the best all-around modern commentary on Genesis is by Gerhard von Rad. His commentary has had its great impact because of its sensitive literary and theological handling of the text. The style is not overly technical, but reflects a highly sophisticated modern exegetical method. Although the author's intent was not directly homiletical, the exposition grapples so well with basic theological issues as to open up the text for the preacher's homiletical use. There are, of course, certain disadvantages to von Rad's book. Often the exegesis rests with an interpretation of the various literary sources without ever treating the text in its final form. Again, the exegesis often presupposes a knowledge of the form critical work of Hermann Gunkel which it seeks to supplement at crucial points. Finally, many traditional questions that have concerned interpreters are not treated by von Rad at all. Thus, in spite of its genuine contribution, even this commentary is quite inadequate for a full treatment of Genesis.

My own suggestion would be to supplement von Rad with a classic exposition from the Reformation period. John Calvin's magnificent Genesis commentary is my first choice. It is one of Calvin's best commentaries and is characterized by its sober attempt to render the literal sense of the book. Martin Luther's lengthy commentary is now available in English, but it is prolix and requires both patience and skill to extract its treasure. However, the enterprise merits the effort involved.

Whether one is teaching or preaching from Genesis, the historical critical issues of modern Biblical studies certainly have to be faced, above all, in respect to the Book of Genesis. Samuel R. Driver's very popular commentary of 1904 remains the best presentation of the critical issues from the perspective of Liberal Protestant theology. Driver lays out the historical, literary, and theological problems raised at the end of the nineteenth century and offers a serious reflection, which, in spite of the change in theological climate, cannot be disregarded. For a full, technical handling of the same issues John Skinner's volume in the *International Critical Commentary* has not been surpassed in English. Of course, Hermann Gunkel's untranslated commentary possesses a brilliance and literary insightfulness which Skinner's volume never attains. One of the more recent critical commentaries is E. A. Speiser's contribution in *The Anchor Bible.* It provides an excellent translation, along with some interesting Ancient Near Eastern parallels. However, usually its theological exposition is quite thin. To most pastors and teachers, probably Nahum M. Sarna's less brilliant volume would prove to be more useful in providing a needed modern historical setting for the book.

A much more theologically conservative approach to the critical questions is represented by Herbert C. Leupold, but, in my judgment, his exegesis is completely dominated by apologetic concerns and shows little expository skill. A more insightful popular commentary from a conservative perspective is that of Derek Kidner. However, by far the most profound commentary from a conservative theological perspective—even if somewhat out-of-date with its mid-nineteenth-century orientation—is that of Franz Delitzsch. His penetration of theological issues and often sensitive handling of the Biblical text is of a high order. Because of constant reference to Hebrew and Arabic, the volume is not light reading, but should challenge the serious student. Delitzsch's commentary should not be confused with Carl F. Keil's volume on the Pentateuch, which has been reprinted. The original German edition of Benno Jacob's commentary is an exhaustive study filled with polemics against Christianity, but nevertheless a profound and often moving illustration of a Jewish understanding of Torah. The recent translation into English of Benno Jacob's commentary is a much abbreviated work of less value, and hardly to be recommended. For anyone interested in working with the Hebrew of Genesis, August Dillmann's old commentary continues to be useful, but George J. Spurrell's *Notes on the Hebrew Text* remains the best choice for the beginner.

There are many books that deal with portions of Genesis. Claus Westermann's huge commentary on Gen., chs. 1 to 11, is much too long-winded for anyone except the specialist, whereas Umberto Cassuto's two volumes on the first part of Genesis through the Abraham stories are to be highly recommended, if used with discernment. In spite of constant apologetic concerns, Cassuto's volumes are filled with insightful observations, some of which border on modern midrash. Alan Richardson's interesting existential interpretation of chs. 1 to 11 is a very creative effort and far excels that of Arthur S. Herbert, whose commentary completes Genesis in the same series. I would recommend that a pastor lead a series of Bible studies on Gen., chs. 1 to 11, using Richardson and Kidner as representative guides into the material. I prefer these volumes to the more recent publication of Robert Davidson. Unfortunately, Walther Zimmerli's stimulating theological commentary on the primeval history remains untranslated. Two highly significant theological treatments of chs. 1 to 3 should not be overlooked. Dietrich Bonhoeffer's *Creation and Fall* and Karl Barth's interpretation in his *Church Dogmatics* III/1 offer profound insights into these basic chapters and have continued to evoke a vigorous reaction. Particularly Bonhoeffer's paperback could form the basis for an excellent church study series. For anyone interested in studying the classic Jewish interpretation of Genesis through the prism of medieval commentaries, the publication of Nehama Leibowitz' *Studies* offers a splendid guide. These lessons have been widely circulated in Israel for two decades and are addressed to a wider audience.

Finally, several homiletical treatments of Genesis should be mentioned. In my judgment, the most helpful volume is by Helmut Thielicke on Gen., chs. 1 to 3. Marcus Dods's famous volume in the *Expositor's Bible* strikes me as being very dated and Victorian in approach, but many have found it useful in the past. Personally I have found the nineteenth-century sermons of Andrew Fuller and Frederick W. Robertson closer to the text, even when the two men represent diametrically opposed interpretations. There are many modern guides to Genesis that are specifically directed to the preacher, but I am not enthusiastic about any. The preacher would be wiser to concentrate his study on the more solid commentaries and avoid the shortcuts. The once highly controversial book of Wilhelm Vischer, *The Witness of the Old Testament to Christ,* was regarded as a major threat to critical exegesis in the 1930's and 1940's even by such Biblical theologians as Eichrodt and von Rad. However, if read as one homiletical model, the interpretation is highly creative and can only serve to stimulate the preacher in serious reflection.

2. Exodus

My first choice for a commentary on Exodus is, naturally, my own volume. The exegesis seeks to interpret the canonical shape of the text and is directed both to the technical problems of the book and to the broader theological use within the Christian church. To what extent it has been successful, I will let the reader decide.

In spite of some reservations I would probably recommend Umberto Cassuto's Exodus commentary as the most useful all-around exposition for the average pastor and teacher. The great strength of the volume lies in its close, sensitive handling of the text. The exegesis is always fresh and highly original. Even though, in my judgment, the exegesis is not up to the level of modern critical scholarship in many respects—Cassuto does not really understand either the literary critical or the form critical method the material that he does offer is not easily found elsewhere. His remarks serve to stimulate further creative reflection on the part of the reader, which is much to be commended. Because the exegesis is very subjective and often idiosyncratic, it should be used with discernment.

Samuel R. Driver's packed little commentary in the *Cam-*

bridge Bible has served as the standard critical English commentary for at least fifty years. In part, this role stemmed from the absence of the Exodus volume in the standard *International Critical Commentary,* but in part it arose from the recognized talents of its author. Driver has filled the volume with critical historical and literary material, all of which reflects his mature and balanced judgment. The Exodus commentary does not open up the text to a homiletical dimension in the same way as does his Genesis, but it contains a mine of useful information. If it can be secured cheaply on the secondhand market, its purchase is certainly recommended. From the outset it has overshadowed the commentary of Alan H. McNeile, which was published shortly before Driver's.

For the advanced student in Old Testament, Bruno Baentsch's companion volume to Gunkel's *Genesis* has long provided a solid, if uninspiring, handling of the technical problems of the Hebrew text. Yet his commentary was very shortly left behind by the brilliant monograph of Hugo Gressmann on Moses which was epoch-making in the development of the form critical method. If one can judge by the first installment, the most recent commentary on Exodus, by Werner H. Schmidt, will become the standard German commentary for the next generation of scholars.

Although there have been a number of recent commentaries in English within the last few years, the choice has not been very promising. Martin Noth's *Exodus* has been important for specialized Exodus research, but as a commentary it has not been successful. On the one hand, because it purports to be a popularization directed to the clergy, it does not treat the technical problems of text criticism or Hebrew philology. On the other hand, its concentration on traditional historical questions leaves most of the important theological issues completely untreated. The more recent volume of James Philip Hyatt is, in my judgment, also basically unsatisfactory. The historical criticism was dated from the outset and did not adequately represent the level of modern form critical and literary research. The theological observations appear thin and rationalistic. Ronald E. Clements' commentary is much to be preferred, but is too abbreviated in its format to offer much help. G. Henton Davies' brief commentary is also disappointing. Then, again, Robert A. Cole's *Exodus,* in the *Tyndale Old*

39

Testament, does not show the exegetical skill of Kidner's companion volume in the same series.

A much more serious attempt at theological exegesis is a commentary by the Catholic scholar James Plastaras. The volume is not a full-blown commentary, but treats most of the major passages in the book and points out the important themes in a creative, theological manner. The book does reflect some of the characteristic emphases of the Biblical Theology Movement of the 1950's, but this has been supplemented with close attention to literary patterns. In spite of a tendency to handle the narrative at times artificially, the commentary can be certainly recommended to both pastor and teacher.

Some of the best exegesis of Exodus has been done in volumes other than the commentary. The best review of modern critical research on the Ten Commandments remains the excellent monograph of Johann Jakob Stamm. This little volume would be of great use to any pastor who was attempting a study series on the Decalogue. However, the classic theological treatments have never been supplemented and remain unexcelled for profound theological reflection on Israel's law. I have in mind particularly the treatment of Aquinas in his *Summa,* Luther in the *Large Catechism,* and Calvin in the *Institutes.* Karl Barth's section in I/2 of the *Church Dogmatics* should also not be overlooked.

Although there has always been a steady stream of books published on the homiletical use of the Ten Commandments, this particular genre of literature quickly becomes dated. These volumes are useful in showing the changing emphases on ethical questions within the church, but will be of little direct assistance to the exegetical efforts of the pastor.

Finally, two paperbacks are highly recommended. Martin Buber's *Moses* is more polemical than some of his other books, but stimulating and original. Walther Zimmerli's *The Law and the Prophets* is a profound theological study of the nature of law in Christian theology, and focuses on the relation of law and prophets in both Testaments. There have been several recent attempts to write biographies of Moses, but without much success.

3. Leviticus

Traditional Christian scholarship has not given much attention to Leviticus except to provide the Old Testament background for New Testament typology. Of course, the contrast of interest for this book in Judaism is striking. In addition, the rise of the historical critical method, particularly in its early stages, contributed to the lack of interest in the book.

As a result, there is not much choice offered in the secondary literature. Several popular works provide basic information, but hardly in such a way as to generate excitement. Norman H. Snaith's commentary offers some insight on Hebrew festivals and sacrifices, but appears quite thin in places. James L. Mays does his best to offer solid theological reflection within the parameters drawn by critical methodology, but he is hampered by the abbreviated format of the series. Martin Noth's commentary, although brilliant and original when dealing with problems of form and tradition criticism, is theologically sterile. Two older volumes which have long served the English clergy, that of Arthur T. Chapman and Annesley W. Streane and that of Archibald R.S. Kennedy, contain much interesting information, particularly the latter commentary, but tend to bog down in the older literary critical issues.

For the modern technical study of Leviticus the student is still much dependent on German commentaries. Bruno Baentsch provides the standard older critical approach with his accustomed learning. Karl Elliger has written a highly technical and over-refined form critical analysis which has not evoked much of a consensus. The thorough commentary of David Hoffmann remains the best exegesis from the perspective of strictly orthodox Judaism and has been reissued in modern Hebrew.

Very little help can be suggested to aid a pastor in the homiletical use of Leviticus. A traditional, Christological exposition by Andrew A. Bonar was once widely used throughout the nineteenth century, but fell into disrepute with the rise of critical scholarship. If used with theological and critical discernment, the book can still be used with profit, in my judgment. Bonar was a very learned scholar deeply immersed in the history of exegesis and he frequently cites the church fathers and the Reformers to

41

good advantage. His book has been recently reprinted in an inexpensive edition.

4. Numbers

The problem in suggesting commentaries for the Book of Numbers is closely akin to that of commentaries for Leviticus. Traditionally among Christians, little attention has been paid to the book. Many of the same authors involved with Leviticus have been assigned Numbers as well. The result is that not a very wide spectrum of opinion is represented.

Popular commentaries are again provided by Norman H. Snaith and James L. Mays. Both the strengths and the weaknesses noted with regard to Leviticus continue to appear in the companion commentaries of Martin Noth, Archibald R. S. Kennedy, and Bruno Baentsch. The commentaries of Leonard Elliott Binns in the *Westminster* series, and Alan H. McNeile in the *Cambridge Bible* were never considered exceptional even when first published, and now appear quite inadequate.

Fortunately, George B. Gray's volume in the *International Critical Commentary* is available for the technical problems of the Hebrew text. This commentary has remained a standard, chiefly because so little detailed work has appeared since 1903 to replace it. However, the general lack of theological interest and many untenable assumptions of the older literary critics disqualify the book from a place high on the priority list of the pastor. It should be noted that some of the better commentaries on Exodus often deal with the narrative material in Numbers.

Finally, Calvin's *Harmony of the Pentateuch,* while usually not included among Calvin's best commentaries, remains a highly useful attempt to relate these parallel passages and should certainly not be overlooked.

5. Deuteronomy

In the light of the great importance of Deuteronomy for the entire Bible, it is surprising to discover that the selection of commentaries is not richer than it is.

In my opinion, the most useful modern commentary is that of Gerhard von Rad. The volume excels in presenting the major literary and the theological problems of Deuteronomy. Still, it r.ust be said that this commentary is far less useful for both scholar and pastor than is his Genesis commentary. The exegesis is far too brief, often merely citing fuller treatments elsewhere, and does not develop the exposition in the length for which von Rad was uniquely equipped.

Samuel R. Driver's famous volume on Deuteronomy in the *International Critical Commentary* has long been considered the standard work in English. Personally I have always come away disappointed when I have used it. Even in the area of Hebrew syntax August Dillmann and Eduard König, among the older commentaries, are more thorough. The strength of Driver's volume lies in the close attention to the literary style and the peculiar vocabulary of the book. The commentary can hardly be considered rich in theological insight.

George Adam Smith's commentary on Deuteronomy has never received the high praise accorded his commentaries on the prophets. Still, in my judgment, his Deuteronomy commentary has been underestimated. The book is tightly packed with technical information, yet its overly terse style makes it difficult to use. It is certainly worth purchasing if it can be bought cheaply on the secondhand market.

There are a good number of popular treatments that are often useful, if not fully satisfactory. George Ernest Wright's contribution in *The Interpreter's Bible* offers a good introduction to Deuteronomy's problems with a serious attempt to see major theological themes. The brief commentaries of Hubert Cunliffe-Jones and Anthony Phillips are too popular to provide any real penetration. John A. Thompson provides a well-informed introduction in which he reviews the present debate in a very adequate fashion. I am far less impressed with the exposition, which is learned but wooden. Peter C. Craigie's commentary is also disappointing in failing to offer much fresh insight. At least he presents a lucid formulation of a traditionally conservative position. For anyone who reads French a much more useful popularization is the volume by Pierre Buis and Jacques Leclercq which is consciously directed to the needs of both priest and laity and tries to communicate the best of modern scholarship.

Several important monographs do supplement the rather meager choice among good commentaries. Gerhard von Rad's *Studies in Deuteronomy* is an exciting volume which has opened up the theological dimensions of the book for a whole generation. It serves to supplement his all too brief commentary. Although von Rad's section on Deuteronomy in his *Old Testament Theology* does not offer much new material, this chapter presents an insightful summary of his interpretation. Adam C. Welch's first monograph on *The Code of Deuteronomy* has been very important in the history of critical scholarship, but from a theological perspective his subsequent volume, *Deuteronomy: The Framework to the Code,* is a profounder theological treatment of the major themes of the book.

For the student interested in the contemporary historical critical debate over the book, Ernest W. Nicholson's monograph *Deuteronomy and Tradition* presents a lucid and reliable review of the past fifty years. Probably the two most important and yet highly controversial monographs of the last decade are Lothar Perlitt's *Bundestheologie im Alten Testament* and Moshe Weinfeld's *Deuteronomy and the Deuteronomic School.* The former contests the antiquity of covenant theology within Israel and defends its seventh-century dating in a way reminiscent of Wellhausen. The latter offers a highly original thesis respecting the "wisdom" influence on Deuteronomy and the role of Jerusalem scribes in its composition. Neither book would be of any immediate use to the pastor.

However, there are two books that can be recommended especially to the pastor. Ronald E. Clements' brief paperback, *God's Chosen People,* is a serious attempt to address the major theological topics in Deuteronomy in the language of the laity and could provide the basis for an adult discussion group. For the thoughtful pastor with a good theological training Luther's important lectures on Deuteronomy should provide much stimulation. Unfortunately, Calvin's *Sermons upon Deuteronomie* remains virtually inaccessible and is available only in the original folio edition of 1584.

6. Joshua

In most series of commentaries the Book of Joshua has been assigned to a scholar who has specialized either in archaeology or in Ancient Near Eastern history. The effect of this selection has been to determine in advance the general shape of most Joshua

44

commentaries. Consequently, it is not surprising that most of the attention of modern commentaries has focused on the historical problems of the book to the exclusion of the literary and theological dimension of the text.

J. Alberto Soggin's recent commentary provides reliable up-to-date information on the geographical and archaeological problems of the text. Considerable attention is also given to the literary critical analysis, still completely within the framework of Martin Noth's theory of Joshua's place within the Deuteronomistic historical work. The theological side of the commentary is inadequately handled, although Soggin is at least aware of this dimension. Another disappointing feature is the failure to deal with the narrative material in a creative way rather than to use it simply as a source for other information.

John Gray's commentary on Joshua is even less satisfactory in terms of theology and literary analysis. The value of his book lies in a significant use of Ancient Near Eastern parallels. The author frequently attempts to reconstruct the original historical event, with varying degrees of success. Above all, the author demonstrates little exegetical skill in illuminating the final form of the Biblical text, but by his consistent referential reading of the text Gray often loses the effect of the narrative. The theological issues are scarcely recognized.

The standard German commentary on Joshua is Martin Noth's highly influential treatment. Although it is obvious that the professional Old Testament scholar must come to grips with Noth's brilliant literary and historical hypotheses, the volume has little to offer the pastor. John Bright's contribution in *The Interpreter's Bible* offers a popular review of Noth's work along with a consistent effort to rebut his interpretation from the more conservative historical position of Albright. In my judgment, it is unfortunate that Hans Wilhelm Hertzberg's commentary on Joshua, Judges, and Ruth remains untranslated. Although this volume is not as successful as his well-known Samuel commentary, it still offers the best combination available of theological, literary, and historical exegesis.

The once-famous commentary on Joshua by John Garstang has not held up well. Because the focus of the author was almost entirely archaeological, the change in interpretation from the early days of Garstang's excavations has rendered the book badly out-of-date. The geographical analysis is still useful, but it must be constantly checked with more recent data. In spite of its conservative attitude toward the historical evidence, the actual exegesis frequently falls back into rather crude rationalistic explanations, such as the crossing of the Jordan by means of an earthquake.

The very recent volume by J. Maxwell Miller and Gene M. Tucker in the *New Cambridge Bible* shows considerable promise at times but suffers from the restrictions of the format. Although the volume by George A. Cooke in the older *Cambridge Bible* series reflected a rather narrow literary interest, nevertheless it did contain two or three times the material of the new addition.

Because of this very one-sided characteristic of most modern commentaries, the serious pastor is thrown back on some of the older volumes in search of a more theologically robust guide. Calvin's final commentary, written just before his death, was on Joshua and is readily available. Carl F. Keil wrote two different commentaries on Joshua which are very conservative and often apologetic. Nevertheless, Keil deals with many traditional problems of a theological nature which are completely avoided by more recent commentators. Finally, William G. Blaikie's homiletical commentary in the *Expositor's Bible* reflects some of the best qualities of the Victorian pulpit and can still be useful for sermon preparation.

7. Judges

Technical commentaries in English on the Book of Judges have been well represented. First of all, George Foot Moore's famous volume in the *International Critical Commentary* has long been regarded as the standard work. In spite of its age the volume is still very useful to the student of the Hebrew Bible for such details as text and philology. From a modern critical point of view, the commentary is badly out-of-date.

Another older technical volume that has long been held in esteem is Charles F. Burney's commentary. Although the approach overlaps somewhat with Moore's commentary, Burney retained his independence and offered a fresh, critical analysis of Judges which supplemented Moore. His careful attention to syntax and the versions still merits attention. However, neither of the two volumes comes to grips with the theological issues in a serious way. At most, one finds a few random remarks on Israel's early, pre-monarchial stage of religious development.

George A. Cooke's commentary in the *Cambridge Bible* again focuses mainly on literary critical problems, but is overshadowed by the larger, more complete commentaries. Cooke makes no real contribution in correcting the theological omission, but occasionally has a fresh observation on the narrative. Arthur E. Cundall uses a modern approach fairly well, but his brief exegesis is very cautious and not overly creative.

The most recent thorough English commentary is Robert G. Boling's in *The Anchor Bible.* The exegesis reflects a modern critical approach from the Albright school. The emphasis falls on historical, archaeological, and textual problems. The exegesis is not easy to read, since it consists of highly technical footnotes to the text. Unfortunately, a serious concern to understand the role of the narrative in its present form is totally lacking. The lapidary comments of the author will serve only to frustrate a pastor seeking to use the Bible as the church's Scripture. Similarly, John Gray's commentary offers some useful information, but in no way fills the need for a serious theological exegesis. For the pastor and the teacher who read German, Hans Wilhelm Hertzberg's commentary probably remains the best resource available. Although Carl F. Keil's old commentary is very dated, I would still recommend its use for providing some help in the areas neglected by modern critical commentaries. Robert A. Watson's homiletical commentary in the *Expositor's Bible* also has an occasional insight.

Specialized monographs on subjects related to the Book of Judges have not provided much help for the pastor to overcome the impasse. John L. McKenzie's *The World of the Judges* popularizes the very kind of background material with which the commentaries are already filled. Kenneth R. R. Gros Louis' essay in *Literary Interpretations of Biblical Narratives* does not offer much penetration into the text. A more promising approach can be found in the beginning chapters of Martin Buber's *The Kingship of God.* However, there is a brilliant little book, virtually unknown in Biblical circles, by Zvi Adar entitled *The Biblical Narrative* which can be highly recommended. Both pastor and teacher will find enormous stimulation in Adar's penetrating analysis of the Samson and Abimelech stories. Finally, it is important for the

Christian pastor to be reminded that Milton was a great Biblical expositor. Such a book as F. Michael Krouse, *Milton's Samson and the Christian Tradition,* serves to recover this often forgotten dimension of Biblical studies.

8. Ruth

The best choice of a commentary in English on the Book of Ruth in unquestionably the recent volume of Edward F. Campbell. His exegesis is extremely thorough and wide-ranging. The textual and philological research is the best available, but carefully distinguished from the exposition itself. The author sets out consciously to do justice to the literary features of the narrative, an aspect that has often been missing in *The Anchor Bible* commentaries. Moreover, it is a welcome surprise to find not only thorough historical background but careful theological reflection throughout the book. Campbell's commentary now completely overshadows the slender popularizations by George A. Cooke and George A. F. Knight.

There are two other well-known essays that a Bible teacher especially could read with great profit. The first is H. H. Rowley's article on Ruth in his collected essays entitled *The Servant of the Lord.* Rowley thoroughly surveys the history of modern research before offering his own comments on the book. The second is the excellent booklet by Ronald M. Hals which explores the book's theology in a fresh way. Less well known but very good is an essay by D. F. Rauber in the volume *Literary Interpretations,* edited by Kenneth R. R. Gros Louis.

I am less impressed with the interpretations of the three recent technical German commentaries on Ruth by Gillis Gerleman, Wilhelm Rudolph, and Ernst Würthwein. Of course, there is much useful information on literary and philological issues, but the overall interpretations are disappointing in their theological penetration. I much prefer the two less technical volumes of Hans Wilhelm Hertzberg and Helmut Lamparter for sensitive, insightful exegesis. The French commentary by Paul Joüon is excellent for its philological notes and rich introduction. It has not been completely superseded by Campbell.

Personally, I have found the recently reprinted homiletical study of Ruth by George Lawson unusable because of its heavy dose of moralism. However, I would recommend Gerhard von Rad's sermon on Ruth, ch. 1, found in his volume of collected sermons.

9. Samuel

Fortunately, the resources for the study of the Books of Samuel are far richer than those available for the rest of the historical books. Hans Wilhelm Hertzberg's commentary on Samuel, although not in the class with von Rad's *Genesis,* is nevertheless a very satisfactory commentary and one of the best in the *Old Testament Library* series. Hertzberg offers a close literary analysis of the Books of Samuel that is theologically sensitive and full of insight. Of particular importance is Hertzberg's concern to relate the historical development of the Biblical tradition to the shaping of the final form of the narrative. Each unit closes with an important analysis of this history. For the pastor preparing a series of sermons or Bible studies on Samuel, Hertzberg's commentary offers an excellent guide.

There are three recent brief commentaries by John Mauchline, William McKane, and Peter R. Ackroyd. Mauchline is a great disappointment and can be safely overlooked. Ackroyd's handling of the text is far more sensitive than McKane's, but he is hampered by a lack of space. Still, these three commentaries have certainly supplanted the older semipopular works of Alexander F. Kirkpatrick *(Cambridge Bible)* and Archibald R. S. Kennedy *(Century Bible).*

For the more technical study of Samuel, again the field is quite well provided. Above all, mention should be made of Samuel R. Driver's *Notes on the Hebrew Text.* This volume does not purport to be a full commentary, but is the finest example in English of the close examination of Hebrew syntax and text criticism. Henry P. Smith's contribution to the *International Critical Commentary* was never considered outstanding and has lost most of its value by now. For the student who handles German, Karl Budde's influential commentary on Samuel remains, along with Julius Wellhausen, a classic example of strictly literary critical analysis. Hugo Gressmann's semipopular commentary represents the early form critical method executed with his usual brilliance. Most recently, Hans Joachim Stoebe's very solid commentary on

I Samuel shows considerable exegetical skill in its handling of the narrative material, but does not achieve the sharp cutting edge one might have expected. Karl Gutbrod's homiletical commentary does a fairly good job of addressing the book from a pastor's perspective, but remains inferior to Hertzberg even for this purpose.

Strictly homiletical commentaries tend to become quickly dated. It is a genuine tribute to their authors that some of the commentaries in the old *Expositor's Bible* series have retained their vitality. In my judgment, William G. Blaikie on Samuel can still be read with profit because he has followed the narrative closely and has resisted, at least in part, the preacher's tendency to moralize on the text. I have not found Andrew W. Blackwood's volume *Preaching from Samuel* very useful, but it is at least an attempt to offer guidance in expository preaching. Unfortunately, Calvin's sermons on I Samuel have never been translated into English.

Although many volumes are available to the preacher on the personality of Biblical characters, in my judgment most of them are very unsatisfactory. The modern authors usually focus on aspects of personality that were foreign to the Biblical narrative. Fleming James's *Personalities of the Old Testament* has long been considered a standard work, and he treats many of the characters in the Book of Samuel. Personally I have never been impressed with his interpretations. However, I do recommend enthusiastically Adam C. Welch's study of *Kings and Prophets*. This is a classic volume, much in the style of the great Scottish Old Testament scholar, Andrew B. Davidson.

10. Kings

There is no one obvious choice of a commentary on Kings. James A. Montgomery's volume in the *International Critical Commentary* is a superb example of text critical scholarship. The historical data is also well handled. However, many of the other qualities that make a superior commentary are missing. The exegesis almost appears to be pre-form critical in its orientation. There is little attempt to treat the narrative material in its literary dimension. Above all, the theological issues fall completely outside the interest and capacity of the author.

I regret deeply that I cannot be enthusiastic over John

Gray's large modern commentary, but it simply does not fill the exegetical need. Of course, the lengthy introduction does provide a useful summary of material, and a fairly reliable review of critical scholarship, but much of this information can be found in any good Bible dictionary. The actual interpretation of the text is thin and idiosyncratic. The author consistently focuses on elements in the text that belong to the background and bypasses the very elements that the Scripture seeks to emphasize (see I Kings, ch. 13).

Charles F. Burney's commentary of 1903 long served as the standard English study of the Hebrew text, but its text critical work has now been superseded by Montgomery's. For the student of Hebrew, Burney's careful attention to syntax and Hebrew idiom will continue to merit its use, although the exegesis itself is largely antiquated.

Two commentaries on Kings appeared in the old *Cambridge Bible* series, the first by Joseph R. Lumby, the second by William E. Barnes. Both are now out-of-date in regard to much technical information, but Lumby's still has some value because of its better handling of the narrative material. The commentary on Kings by Joseph Robinson in the latest edition of the *Cambridge Bible* is rather thin on commentary and weak in theological insight. Another commentary on Kings of approximately the same age and format as the earlier *Cambridge Bible* series is John Skinner's small volume in the *Century Bible*. Skinner's reputation for solid, careful interpretation is sustained throughout the commentary and he managed to pack much useful interpretation into this slender volume.

For the professional scholar and the advanced student there are several important commentaries in German. Unfortunately, Martin Noth's much anticipated commentary has been left uncompleted by his untimely death. It is now apparent that considerable time will elapse before the enterprise will be completed by his successor, Rudolf Smend. Also the very learned commentary of Albert Šanda is a splendid example of pre-Vatican II, conservative Catholic scholarship. It contains a wealth of solid exposition which has often been overlooked. In addition to this technical research there is an outstanding commentary directed to the pastor by Johannes Fichtner on I Kings. It would be a great service if this commentary were translated, since it offers an excellent combination of literary skill and theological understanding, which has always been rare. Following Fichtner's death the volume on II Kings was prepared by Klaus Dietrich Fricke. The commentary is also good, but does not reach the level of Fichtner.

There are some very useful homiletical guides for the serious pastor who has some insight and perseverance in recovering buried treasure. Karl C. W. F. Baehr's commentary in the old J. P. Lange series is one of the few examples of that vintage which merits attention. The homiletical suggestions are often full of imagination and promise. In addition, Frederic W. Farrar's commentary in the *Expositor's Bible* abounds in Victorian rhetoric, but is a rich and vigorous exposition from that age. Moreover, the sermons of Frederick D. Maurice, *The Prophets and Kings of the Old Testament,* are not without a certain charm. Once again, Carl F. Keil's commentary often surprises the reader with a profound theological insight.

Fortunately, creative homiletical exegesis is not confined to antiquarian volumes. Jacques Ellul's brilliant interpretation in *The Politics of God and the Politics of Man* can be recommended with enthusiasm to the pastor. Obviously, his interpretation is often subjective and at times even fanciful, but Ellul offers a bold and creative mode for serious exposition of Kings. Of a similar genre and equal in brilliance is the lengthy exposition of I Kings, ch. 13, by Karl Barth in II/2 of *Church Dogmatics.*

One final word may be in order regarding the subject of chronology which plays such a major role in the Book of Kings. I certainly regard Edwin R. Thiele's study *The Mysterious Numbers of the Hebrew Kings* as a serious book which is packed with useful information on the complex problems of chronology in Israel and the Ancient Near East. However, I do not regard his elaborate system to be a correct interpretation of the Biblical data, and I would argue that Thiele's exegetical method ultimately fails to understand the canonical function of chronology. Still, for those interested in this aspect of the Book of Kings, Thiele's book offers one of the few introductions available in English.

11. Chronicles

Less attention has been afforded Chronicles than the other historical books. Only rather recently in the periodical literature have the theological possibilities of the Chronicler begun to be explored. Few commentaries have been able to sustain a high level of interest throughout.

Jacob M. Myers' rather recent commentary of two volumes in *The Anchor Bible* is usually regarded as the best modern choice. Myers handles the technical problems of text and historical background quite well. His chief interest and competence focus on the contribution from recent archaeological work. In this regard his commentary usually supplants the older, standard *International Critical Commentary* volume of Edward L. Curtis. However, if Myers' commentary is compared with the leading German commentary of Wilhelm Rudolph, it does not measure up to the best of Continental scholarship. In actual interpretation, Myers demonstrates little exegetical skill, and the theological issues are often handled in a superficial way.

In my opinion, the pastor would do better to work with the commentary of Peter R. Ackroyd. In spite of the brevity of the work, Ackroyd's exegesis is exciting and fully abreast of the recent recovery of the Chronicler's important theological role. Of course, Ackroyd's popular treatment needs to be supplemented with a more detailed commentary. My own choice would be Carl F. Keil rather than William A. L. Elmslie in the *Cambridge Bible* series. A reader who is aware of Keil's apologetic concerns and uses the exegesis critically will find it invaluable as a very learned and carefully argued commentary, which defends a traditional orthodox Protestant position. A comparison of Keil with Otto Zöckler's commentary in the J. P. Lange series of about the same age will confirm the clear superiority of Keil, who is at his best in this material.

By and large, the German commentaries on Chronicles are somewhat superior to those in English, when judged from the perspective of critical research. Mention has already been made of Wilhelm Rudolph's very detailed and enormously learned commentary. In my judgment, this is Rudolph's finest commentary, and his meticulous research in this difficult area has placed Old Testament scholarship in his debt. Then again, I still hold the older commentary of Ernst Bertheau in esteem. His detailed scrutiny of the Hebrew text has never been fully superseded, and much of value remains for the advanced student. Conversely, I have not found the elaborate commentary of Johann W. Rothstein very helpful, particularly since the exegesis was discontinued after I Chronicles. Finally, Kurt Galling's more popular commentary does not commend itself greatly. It lacks the detail of Rudolph, but has not contributed much in theological insight for which this particular series *(Das Alte Testament Deutsch)* was designed. In many ways the semipopular commentary of Johann Goettsberger is much more successful in communicating the major themes of the book, and should be better known than it is.

For the serious advanced student of the Bible the work of Gerhard von Rad on Chronicles deserves special mention. His important monograph in 1930, *Das Geschichtsbild des Chronistischen Werkes,* initiated the revived interest in the Chronicler. In his brilliant article, translated into English as "The Levitical Sermon in I and II Chronicles," one can catch a glimpse of some important moves that are immediately relevant to the homiletical use of the Biblical tradition.

12. Ezra and Nehemiah

The commentary situation in regard to the Book of Ezra and the Book of Nehemiah is closely parallel to that of Chronicles. Many of the same authors are involved, with their commentaries showing similar strengths and weaknesses.

The standard technical volume of the *International Critical Commentary* by Loring W. Batten is old and much out-of-date regarding critical matters, but nevertheless for a detailed study of text and Hebrew grammar the volume has retained a certain value. Clearly this commentary was not one of the outstanding contributions in the series, but it was generally competent for that period. The lack of any real theological discernment reduces its worth greatly for the pastor.

Jacob M. Myers has written the commentary on Ezra and Nehemiah for *The Anchor Bible,* and it follows very much the lines of his Chronicles. Once again, in terms of technical scholarship as well as a theological grasp his commentary is not in the same class with Wilhelm Rudolph's German commentary. Peter R. Ackroyd's brief comments on Ezra and Nehemiah are often stimulating, but do not go into the needed detail. Unfortunately, Leonard H. Brockington's recent contribution is very disappointing, focusing solely on historical problems and showing little feel for literary or theological issues. The commentary is poorly organized and at times idiosyncratic. Herbert E. Ryle's little commentary in the *Cambridge Bible* offers the standard literary critical analysis of that period without much flair or originality.

Again my advice would be to use Carl F. Keil's commentary for its solid, thorough Hebrew scholarship. Its strength lies in his attempt to understand the present canonical shaping of the book in the light of traditional Christian exegesis. However, Keil consistently harmonizes tensions in the text which, as part of the canonical witness, should not be resolved by a rationalistic move from either the left or the right of the theological spectrum. For the student who reads German, Ernst Bertheau's older commentary offers a good check on Keil.

It is of interest to note that, whereas traditional Christian exegesis did not pay much attention to Chronicles, interest in Ezra and especially in Nehemiah was always strong. Each generation produced homiletical treatments of Nehemiah, who was seen as a model of faith in adversity. Much of this sermonic material fell as a casualty to the historical critical approach of the late nineteenth century which generally denigrated the period. Perhaps this is the time to attempt a recovery of this material for robust preaching. I only regret that there is no good homiletical model in English to recommend. In German, Walter Lüthi's sermons on Nehemiah's rebuilding of destroyed Jerusalem which were directed to the Europe of post-World War II remain powerful expository examples of strong Biblical preaching.

13. Esther

Esther is an Old Testament book that has lived on the very edges of the Christian canon from the outset. This ambiguous evaluation is in striking contrast to the book's high esteem among Jews. Although sufficient exegetical helps are available for the serious student of this book, the search for its theological role within the life of the church is far from settled and remains a continuing challenge to the modern pastor.

The technical problems of the book—philological, literary, and historical—are well handled by Lewis B. Paton in the standard *International Critical Commentary*. His contribution is certainly one of the strongest volumes in this series and has not received the commendation it deserves. Paton offers the most thorough treatment of the history of exegesis available and his knowledge of Jewish exegesis is impressive. Conversely, Carey A. Moore's recent contribution in *The Anchor Bible* is disappointing. His interpretation, in my judgment, lacks real penetration, is often flippant, and contributes little beyond Paton.

Modern technical commentaries are also well represented in German by Max Haller, Gillis Gerleman, Hans Bardtke, and Ernst Würthwein. Bardtke's is the longest and the most thorough study. He attempts a brief theological evaluation which, however, is quite meager. His separate monograph on Luther and the Book of Esther is a much stronger theological contribution. Gerleman has made a significant attempt to relate Esther to the Exodus traditions, although it appears somewhat strained. Some of the parallels from the history of religions are useful to the scholar. Würthwein's commentary is all too brief. For the strictly literary qualities of Esther, Hermann Gunkel's classic study remains unsurpassed even by the most recent monograph of Werner Dommershausen.

Of the more popular commentaries, Bernhard W. Anderson's contribution in *The Interpreter's Bible* at least tries to recover a theological dimension, although the format of the series consistently hampers serious exegesis. Annesley W. Streane in the *Cambridge Bible* is still quite informative, even if not always profound. George A. F. Knight's work is less impressive on Esther and much too brief. The same judgment can be made of Helmer Ringgren. Most of the older conservative commentators, such as Carl F. Keil, have bogged down in an elaborate defense of the book's historicity without providing much illumination of the text itself. Johannes Schildenberger's German commentary is also a representative of this apologetic genre.

In my judgment, the most serious theological interpretation of Esther remains Wilhelm Vischer's brilliant little essay of 1937 directed to the Christian church living under the threat of Nazi anti-Semitism. Few will agree with Vischer at all points, and many will reject his interpretation out-of-hand, but I recommend it as a profound and highly creative attempt to come to grips with anti-Semitism in the light of the Book of Esther.

14. Job

The Book of Job is well furnished with good commentaries in English. This remark is not to suggest for a moment that a consensus on the interpretation of the book has appeared or that most of the hard exegetical questions have been finally resolved. Rather, there is a wide spectrum of serious interpretation represented, and excellent guides are available by which the pastor and the teacher can pursue their own study of this magnificent book. Because of the enormous richness and complexity of the Book of Job one should work with several different volumes since no one commentary, however excellent, can excel at all points.

There are several unusually thorough technical commentaries which are indispensable for the pastor who is working with the Hebrew. The volume of Samuel R. Driver and George B. Gray in the *International Critical Commentary* offers the most thorough handling of the philological problems, but in a somewhat dull manner. Edouard Dhorme's huge commentary is a model of its kind in the exhaustive handling of the textual problems. His introductory essays are very illuminating and his analysis of the theological themes of the book is of great value. However, his actual exposition of the text in the body of the commentary is brief and disappointing. Marvin H. Pope's recent commentary in *The Anchor Bible* offers a vigorous, fresh translation. His lengthy introduction provides a reliable survey of the field of scholarship, and his careful use of recent comparative material, particularly from Ugaritic, commends itself. Form critical research is best found in Georg Fohrer's large German commentary, but its success in illuminating the Book of Job has not been overwhelming. I have found nothing of particular merit in Gustav Hölscher's commentary that has not been covered by one of the larger volumes.

Because of the unusual difficulty in understanding the language of Job, it is natural that the technical commentaries have tended to get lost in a myriad of small problems. For that reason some of the best exposition of the book as a whole is found in the less technical commentaries. In fact, I would strongly advise the pastor and the student to start building their library from books of this category and then later to strengthen their resources from the technical commentaries whenever needed.

In many ways the great classic in English has remained Andrew B. Davidson's commentary in the old *Cambridge Bible*. The great value of the book is in its lucid, sober analysis of the literal sense of the text without constantly intruding a host of scholarly theories into the discussion. Davidson sees most of the exegetical problems and he faces them as honestly as possible. Moreover, there is a profound theological wrestling with the book throughout his exegesis which provides his work with an enduring richness. Since this volume can be secured easily on the secondhand-book market, I would suggest that it be part of a minister's library.

I would next mention Franz Delitzsch's commentary as one of the other great old classics. Delitzsch's two-volume work can hardly be called a popularization. Indeed, its frequent reference to the cognate languages makes it difficult to use. However, even though much of the philological work is now out-of-date and can be passed over, the exposition itself is often profound and moving. His commentary continues to warrant close study and is also readily available in an inexpensive reprint.

In addition, among older semipopular works the commentaries of Samuel Cox, Arthur S. Peake, James Strahan, and Edgar C. S. Gibson, each representing differing positions, have long been used by pastors with great profit. Particularly valuable is the packed little volume by Peake, which is inexpensive and easy to obtain secondhand.

Among the more recent popular commentaries on Job, mention should first be made of the vigorously theological exegesis of Samuel Terrien. In my judgment, his existential interpretation overlooks important dimensions in the book, but undoubtedly his approach has brought into clear focus an important quality of the dialogues. H. H. Rowley's commentary, one of his last works, is a solid, reliable guide to recent scholarly discussion of the book, but it can be safely bypassed. In my judgment, probably the finest popular commentary is the brilliant theological exposition of Helmut Lamparter, as yet untranslated. Lamparter, who is virtually unknown in the English-speaking world, has unusual gifts as a sensitive interpreter of Scripture. His contributions are by far the best in this otherwise rather unimpressive series. At least I greatly prefer Lamparter to Artur Weiser's much better known volume.

As one would expect, there continues to be a steady stream of monographs on interpreting various aspects of the Book of Job. Generally I would avoid purchasing this type of volume. Many of them are engaged in defending some idiosyncratic theory of composition, and when once read in the library, need not be referred to as a lasting resource. Perhaps one exception would be the stimulating paperback of Nahum N. Glatzer entitled *The Dimensions of Job.* This book contains an excellent collection of essays on Job representing the widest possible range of opinions. I would not advise its use in a church Bible class lest the class be distracted into peripheral issues far from the text itself, but in other contexts the volume has great value. The book also provides a good introduction into classic Jewish interpretation of Job which is contrasted with traditional Christian understanding.

There are numerous models for the preacher to study on the homiletical use of Job. Gregory's famous sermons, used by the Christian church for a thousand years as the major guide into the book, are probably too far removed from the modern age in spirit to be of much aid. Still, Gregory should remain a challenge to the modern preacher to do as well for his congregation as Gregory did for his! A small selection of Calvin's sermons on Job are available in English translation. Again, not to be overlooked is the fascinating interpretation of Job offered by Karl Barth in four lengthy sections in IV/3 of his *Church Dogmatics.* Wilhelm Vischer's untranslated study of Job has left a powerful impact on a generation of German- and French-speaking pastors. Although I personally do not look with much favor on the modern psychological interpretation of the book, at least mention should be made of Carl Jung's famous book *Answer to Job* and H. Wheeler Robinson's *The Cross in the Old Testament.*

15. Psalms

No book in the Old Testament has been more important to the life of the Christian church than the Psalter. No book offers more richness and challenge to the pastor. Yet no book requires of its modern reader greater skill and theological reflection in order to tap its enormous resources successfully. Obviously any pastor's library that is not well supplied in a variety of different volumes on the Psalms is sorely deficient.

Where to begin? The opinion is widely held that the historical critical approach to the Bible has rendered works on the Psalter prior to the late nineteenth century largely invalid, and that therefore one needs to begin with a critical introduction that sets out the advances in method afforded by modern form criticism before listing the modern critical commentaries. I do not share this opinion. In my judgment, it has resulted in a disastrous reductionism for theology, liturgy, and preaching. Rather, I would argue that each period—of course including the modern critical period—has made its peculiar contribution, and that these differing expositions all need to be critically assessed. The real issue is between good and bad interpretation, both of which have been represented throughout the history of the church.

My own reason for beginning with the modern period is that this avenue into the literature is more easily accessible to the average pastor. It does not imply a greater importance, nor does it suggest that the building of a library should begin with modern commentaries.

There are many introductions into the modern critical study of the Psalms. I would advise purchasing few of this type of book because any good modern commentary will rehearse the same issues. Nevertheless one or two inexpensive booklets would be useful. I would probably choose Christoph Barth's inexpensive paperback or the solid introduction of Pius Drijvers. Both are greatly superior to Helmer Ringgren's *The Faith of the Psalmists*. Of course, Hermann Gunkel's own discussion of his form critical method is available in an inexpensive pamphlet. In my opinion, Sigmund Mowinckel's two-volume introduction should concern only the professional scholar, since its effect on actual exegesis is, at best, indirect.

Turning now to the selection of a modern commentary, I confess my dissatisfaction with the options available. This comment is not to suggest that little of value is found in the modern commentary, but rather that no one commentary can be judged an adequate guide. There is a wide consensus that the *International Critical Commentary* volume of Charles A. Briggs is virtually unusable because of the peculiar theories of meter that dominated the interpretation of the author. Of course Briggs's comments on Hebrew grammar are still useful, but much of this information can be easily found elsewhere. Mitchell Dahood's three-volume commentary in *The Anchor Bible* has evoked a heated controversy from the outset. Space is too limited for a detailed review. In my own judgment, the commentary reflects a major hermeneutical confusion between treating the Psalter as misunderstood vestiges of Ugaritic poetry or as the Scriptures of the church and the synagogue. I can only conclude that the average pastor will be hopelessly confused by this commentary and that Dahood's exegesis should be left to the professionals to debate.

The two best options among the modern critical commentaries in English are the volumes of Artur Weiser and Arnold A. Anderson. Weiser's treatment is the profounder, in my judgment. It is form critically oriented and theologically alert. Yet the exegesis suffers from Weiser's peculiar theories of a covenant festival, which often reduces the value of the interpretation. Anderson's volume has been generally well received. It offers a lucid, well-organized survey of modern opinion on each psalm and a balanced judgment typical of English commentaries which eschews extremes. The exegesis is sensible throughout, but also derivative. I have not included Edward J. Kissane's commentary as a modern option because it is out of print and somewhat idiosyncratic in method.

There are several older commentaries from the pre-form critical period which if used with discretion are invaluable. My first choice among the older English commentaries is John J. S. Perowne's much-used set. This exegesis represents the best of nineteenth-century Anglican tradition. Its strength lies in its close attention to the Hebrew text along with careful scrutiny of the Septuagint. The writer has a good knowledge of the history of exegesis and a profound sense of the unity of the two Testaments. This set provides an excellent balance to the modern commentaries which seldom deal with the New Testament's use of the Psalter. Another very solid volume of a slightly later period, but in the same general tradition, is by Alexander F. Kirkpatrick. The volume is closely packed with information and is more historically oriented than Perowne's. Also, the theological penetration is slightly less evident in Kirkpatrick. Finally, mention should be made of Franz Delitzsch's three-volume commentary. Much of the material in the commentary is out-of-date, but other aspects such as his attention to the Masoretic system of accents are without a close rival. The interpretation is sometimes heavy, but has

61

a profundity that continues to challenge its serious reader. I am less than enthusiastic over the commentaries of William O. E. Oesterley and William E. Barnes. The history of Israel's religion has, by and large, replaced serious theological reflection, and much of the inherent vitality in the language of the Psalter has been drained of its power. Also I would not recommend Ernst W. Hengstenberg for the opposite reason: he confuses apologetics with exposition.

Brief notice should be taken of the various German commentaries, because they have played such an important role in the history of Biblical studies. Hermann Gunkel's large commentary was epoch-making in its pioneer development of the form critical method. In spite of the fact that theology has been replaced by aesthetics, the exposition is clearly that of a master and has no rival in terms of literary sensitivity. Hans-Joachim Kraus's equally large commentary is significant in its attempt to use Gunkel's form critical method in the service of the Christian church. Each psalm is subjected to a detailed critical analysis, but concludes with a traditional homily, usually taken from Luther or Calvin. Quite obviously the relationship between Kraus's critical methodology and his theological position remains in great tension. Finally, Helmut Lamparter's popular commentary is often insightful for the pastor, but is not as successful as his Job commentary. Also intended for the pastor, and available in French or German, is Alfons Deissler's popular exposition which represents the "anthological" style of the great French Catholic scholar, André Robert.

Probably the gravest indictment against the historical critical method is that it has effectively blocked all access to the richness of pre-critical interpretation of the Bible, both Jewish and Christian. To some extent the church's liturgical use of the Old Testament Psalms has been able to survive the impact of critical exegesis. In my judgment, it is absolutely imperative for the serious and theologically robust use of the Psalms once again to regain this lost heritage. Obviously traditional forms cannot be simply repristinated in the post-critical age, but neither can the great giants of the past be simply ignored without serious impoverishment of the Christian church.

At the head of any list stands the *Enarrationes* of Augustine, still available in an inexpensive reprint. Augustine provided the prism through which the Psalter was refracted during the larger part of Christian history. The exposition is not easy reading and runs counter to everything that the historical critical method assumes as obvious. Augustine does not interpret the text to discover what the Biblical author originally meant, but he replays the chords of the text as one plays an organ in order to orchestrate one's praise to the God and Father of Jesus Christ. The exposition is not for beginners, but for the serious pastor who wrestles with Scripture in a search for the presence of God. Along with Augustine the commentary of Jerome probably should be mentioned, but there is no comparison in the profundity of the two.

Any pastor and teacher interested in the history and development of Christian liturgy should not overlook the great collection of church fathers and medieval writers on the Psalter which has been assembled by John M. Neale and Richard F. Littledale in four volumes. Once again, entry into this material is not easy, but it is a field eminently worthy of being explored. For example, if one were to contrast any one form of medieval hymnology with that of Isaac Watts in the use of the Psalter, both the contrasts and the similarities would be of great interest.

The Reformation produced a whole cluster of superb commentaries on the Psalms. In my judgment, Calvin's commentary on the Psalter is one of his most magnificent achievements. Of course, anyone who reads Calvin with Gunkel's questions will come away disappointed. However, the pastor or the teacher with the theological maturity to discern Calvin's questions will soon be caught up by the sheer brilliance of this exposition. Equally impressive, but very different, is Luther's commentary, some selected portions of which have been republished in the American edition. For the pastor who is trying to understand the Psalms from the vantage point of Good Friday and Easter, no better guide can be found than Luther's exposition of the Penitential Psalms.

Much of the best of Puritan exegesis was done in relation to the Psalter. I would call to your attention the names of John Owen, Richard Baker, Richard Sibbes, and Henry Ainsworth as just a few of the great expositors. David Dickson, whose lovely commentary has been recently reprinted, belongs in the same company. The exegesis is warm, vigorous, bold, and devotional and is highly recommended. Charles H. Spurgeon's once-famous *Treasury of David* still provides a reliable guide into the Puritan period.

Standing outside the perimeter of Christian tradition but

serving as a major source of edification were the great Jewish interpreters of the Psalms. It is greatly welcomed that another portion of Rabbi David Kimḥi's famous commentary has appeared in a recent English translation by Joshua Baker and Ernest W. Nicholson. Also, special attention should be paid to William G. Braude's excellent translation, *The Midrash of Psalms.* This two-volume work is the best guide into the heart of Jewish understanding of the Psalms and retains great value for Christian theology as well.

Finally, there are innumerable models for the sermonic use of the Psalms. Augustine's *Selected Sermons* presents a totally different genre from his commentary and is immediately accessible. John Donne's *Sermons on the Psalms and Gospels* has been reprinted because of his unparalleled use of the English language. Both are profound and moving. Alexander Maclaren's exposition in the *Expositor's Bible* provides a rather good example of strong Victorian preaching. Lastly, Dietrich Bonhoeffer's reflections on the Psalms remain an impressive testimony to a modern devotional appropriation.

16. Proverbs

Only rather recently have the wide theological implications of Israel's wisdom literature for the life of the Christian church been again rediscovered. Several generations of scholars had left the impression that the Proverbs belonged on the edge of the canon and were secular rather than religious. Of course, this misunderstanding was not shared in the Reformation and post-Reformation periods, as evidenced by the extensive exegetical attention paid to Proverbs by such illustrious persons as Philip Melanchthon, Martin Geier, John Mercerus, John Cocceius, and John Maldonatus. It is therefore exciting to see the renewed growth of theological interest in the Proverbs. For the modern pastor or teacher who still is at a loss in dealing with the Proverbs, I would suggest as an exciting introduction Gerhard von Rad's book *Wisdom in Israel.* Even when his discussion does not evoke full agreement, it cannot fail to stimulate the serious student to renewed reflection on the nature of wisdom.

There are several very readable modern commentaries that also can provide help in interpretation. Robert B. Y. Scott's volume in *The Anchor Bible* is very lucid and illuminating in its introduction, but a bit thin in the exposition itself. William O. E. Oesterley's commentary, although somewhat old by now, was one of the best contributions in the *Westminster* series and is still very useful. Except for problems in Hebrew philology, the exegesis is usually superior to that of Crawford H. Toy in the *International Critical Commentary*. My impression of the latest technical commentary, by William McKane, is very mixed. McKane has brought much learning to bear on his study, and most students will learn from his lengthy introduction. Yet the exegesis itself is disappointing. The exegesis is dominated by a larger theory respecting the development of Israel's wisdom which I judge to be untenable. McKane envisions a growth from an early nontheological stage of simple empirical observation to a subsequent growth of "God language." The effect of these rigid categories is to rob the proverbs of much of their theological vitality.

I recommend with much more enthusiasm the older commentary of Franz Delitzsch. Here Delitzsch is at his best, and the exegesis is far less dated than his work on the Psalms and the Prophets. However, unless one does handle Hebrew, much of the strength of the exposition is lost. Of the two recent popular commentaries by Derek Kidner and R. Norman Whybray, I prefer the sensible, balanced comments of Kidner, who has packed much wisdom into this slender commentary.

For the advanced student or teacher who handles languages other than English, mention should be made of Berend Gemser's standard commentary in German which is of high exegetical quality, particularly from a form critical perspective, and André Barucq's learned French commentary. Again, Helmut Lamparter has written an exciting homiletical commentary which has been much criticized, but is still of great interest for its originality. The author attempts to arrange all the proverbs under the rubrics provided by the Decalogue. Even if this move involves a *tour de force,* his attempt to bring the proverbs in close relationship to the rest of the canon has been done with genuine theological insight.

Finally, mention should be made of Charles Bridges's thoroughly Victorian commentary, recently reprinted. The exposition abounds in quaint moralisms which often are far removed from the Biblical world. Nevertheless, there are moments of genuine insight, and for the pastor who has flexibility in his theological approach the exposition may serve as catalyst to stimulate his own homiletical reflection.

17. Ecclesiastes

Few books in the Old Testament have been more neglected by modern preachers or dismissed by teachers as the curious musings of a gentle cynic. Yet this was the same book that once had inspired many of the church fathers and most of the early Reformers to write full commentaries and preach countless sermons. I do not propose any easy way by which to recover the church's understanding of the book as Scripture; rather, I would agree with Christian David Ginsburg that it is far easier to chronicle the history of the book's demise. Nevertheless, I would sincerely hope that a new chapter can be written which will again testify to the impact of this book on the life of the church.

Perhaps the best way to proceed would be to work at the same time with both newer and older commentaries. From the modern research one can profit from the new knowledge of Israel's language, history, and institutions. From the older commentaries one can again seek to appreciate the various theological possibilities of this material within a community of faith. Incidentally, James Strong offers the most thorough bibliography of all the older resources.

Of the modern commentaries, Robert B. Y. Scott's is clear and informative on modern literary and historical research, even if the actual interpretation is too brief to answer the more difficult questions. Roland E. Murphy's succinct comments in the *Jerome Biblical Commentary* are illuminating and perceptive. A. Lukyn Williams' commentary is also a serious contribution. Then again, good use can be made of Robert Gordis' well-known commentary. His exegesis is far richer than Scott's and he sets the book within the broader context of Israel's sapiential traditions of the Persian and Hellenistic periods. His close attention to the Biblical idiom is exceedingly valuable, as are his rabbinic parallels. Still, I find unsatisfactory Gordis' constant recourse to cultural and psychological factors by which to explain the book's peculiar contours. He ends by blunting the sharp edges of the theological issues.

Among the more technical commentaries one can find all

the various approaches of modern critical research well represented. Edouard Podechard is outstanding for text criticism and close literary analysis. George A. Barton is competent but hardly outstanding. Kurt Galling offers the most thorough form critical study and history of traditions.

However, the impression should certainly not be given that theological interest in Ecclesiastes is lacking among all the modern commentaries. In German there are at least two notable exceptions. Walther Zimmerli's commentary makes a sustained effort to wrestle with the theological dimension of the book within the ongoing wisdom traditions. His comments are quite brief, but always perceptive. However, in my judgment, the second edition of Hans Wilhelm Hertzberg's commentary is the most impressive of the newer commentaries. In addition to a thorough discussion of the Hebrew text, he has appended a twenty-five-page essay on the theology of Koheleth which is both insightful and profound.

If one now turns to the older commentators, one cannot help observing how strikingly different the theological issues were handled. Ernst W. Hengstenberg's volume on Ecclesiastes is probably his best commentary and still shares some robust features of the Reformers' reading of the book. Of course, Hengstenberg's style is polemical and tendentious, but in his handling of the epilogue of the book one senses how very different was his understanding of the theological role of the canon even in comparison with Zimmerli. In addition, Delitzsch, whose position is far removed from Hengstenberg's, nevertheless ascribes a strong positive theological role to the book and his commentary is highly recommended.

In many ways, my favorite English commentary is the rich little volume of Edward H. Plumptre in the first edition in the old *Cambridge Bible.* Plumptre was a scholar and churchman of great wisdom. The author was immersed in the Patristic commentators as well as in the Greek and Roman classics, which he cites to great advantage. His appendix on Koheleth in Shakespeare and Tennyson is marvelous.

Finally, I would strongly advise the serious pastor to begin work in the commentaries of the Reformers themselves. Johann Brenz's commentary of 1528 has been recently republished and a new edition of Martin Bucer's works has been announced.

Obviously the first choice falls to the excellent new English translation of Luther's commentary. Certainly here is the place for the pastor to begin in rethinking the role of Ecclesiastes.

Lest one too easily restrict the theological issues to those of Luther, I would also suggest as a good Reformed anecdote the use of Wilhelm Vischer's provocative essay on Ecclesiastes, the brief comments of Karl Barth in III/4 of the *Church Dogmatics,* and the excellent sermons of Walter Lüthi.

18. Song of Songs

No book of the Old Testament has caused greater problems for the interpreter than has the Song of Songs. Franz Delitzsch characterized it flatly as "the most obscure book of the Old Testament." The history of interpretation of the book reflects several different hermeneutical approaches, including the allegorical, typological, and naturalistic, as well as strikingly different evaluations of the literary forms of the book such as allegory, parable, drama, and lyrical poems. Because of this great variety of interpretation, it is very difficult to evaluate commentaries. However, it seems to me unwise to limit the suggestions of commentaries to some one theory of interpretation, since no unanimity has emerged within the church regarding its canonical function. Rather, I would prefer to leave the hermeneutical issue open, and seek to distinguish between good and bad interpretations within this wide spectrum of differing opinions.

The allegorical interpretation of the Song has long been represented within the church. Persons trained in the historical critical method usually have rejected this approach immediately as untenable. Indeed, its weakness has always been in the difficulty of controlling the element of subjectivity when the interpretation is admittedly not derived from the literal sense. Several allegorical interpretations in the English language have been widely used for preaching, particularly in the nineteenth century. These would include the commentaries of John Gill, George Burrowes, and A. Moody Stuart. In my judgment, it would be better for a modern preacher to study the father of the allegorical commentary, Origen, than his less gifted imitators. Origen's commentary is readily available in an English translation.

The dramatic interpretation of the Song construes it as a

type of play with a plot and a series of actors. The key to this interpretation turns both on the correct division of the scenes and on the proper determination of the characters. The two major commentaries in English translation representing this position are the commentaries of Franz Delitzsch and Otto Zöckler. Delitzsch's interpretation is the more convincing, but it labors under the enormous handicap of trying to develop a scenario that cannot be clearly traced in the text itself. Consequently, Delitzsch's work on the Song is generally regarded as his least convincing commentary. A popular variation of this approach, based originally upon the research of Johann Jakob Wettstein, sought to reconstruct from the Song the different parts of a seven-day marriage ceremony. Different songs were then assigned to the various participants. Karl Budde's German commentary is the classic representative of this theory, but it has been frequently popularized in English.

Beginning in the nineteenth century a cultic interpretation of the Song has been defended by commentators, especially by those who would connect the book with pagan festivals. Theophile J. Meek in *The Interpreter's Bible* and Helmer Ringgren among others are representatives of this approach. Neither one's commentary is very illuminating. The exegesis strains to find elements in the text that at best lie well below the surface.

Certainly the most popular interpretation is one which holds that the Song of Songs is comprised of a collection of love poems. Yet among the various interpreters there is considerable difference in the manner in which this position is developed. Gillis Gerleman suggests that once this correct literary analysis has been made there is little of theological significance to add. Robert Gordis, however, while also defending the songs as being secular love songs, seeks to explore the significance of their inclusion within the canon. His comments are enriched by constant reference to rabbinic interpretation. Wilhelm Rudolph and Ernst Würthwein both provide more theological substance than Gerleman, but the focus of the commentaries falls on other features of the text without much sustained reflection on the theological issues. In spite of the brevity of the actual exegesis, George A. F. Knight's introduction in the *Torch Bible* provides an unusually rich theological study. His commentary can be warmly recommended as providing a good start. Again, Helmut Lamparter develops the interpretation of secular love songs in a creative theological manner. Finally, Andrew Harper's slender volume in the *Cambridge Bible* is of high quality and offers a reliable guide to the text.

Quite a different approach to the love song theory is found in the French commentary of Denis Buzy. He argues that the songs always spoke of sacred love and therefore were intended to be understood metaphorically. The love songs functioned as an extended parable to illustrate the covenant relationship between God and his people. Buzy has argued his case with great learning and insight and it is deserving of close study even by those who do not share his approach.

Finally, mention should be made of the "anthological" approach to the Song represented by André Robert and André Feuillet. By means of several monographs and then a massive commentary these scholars have argued the case for understanding the text as a highly sophisticated compilation of midrashic allusions to other sacred texts of Scripture, particularly from the prophets. Seen in this light, the Song of Songs offers a prophetic interpretation of Israel's relationship to God. I have found Robert's commentary rich and stimulating, but not fully convincing. Again the author is pushing an interpretation that is not immediately evident from the text itself. As a result the theological concern of the book emerges blurred and confused. In my judgment, the earlier exegesis of Feuillet in 1953 makes a more convincing case for the method than the full-blown commentary of 1963.

To summarize: The pastor has at his disposal various resources that can be of great aid, but the basic task of illuminating this book as Scripture of the church for today remains a challenge still to be met.

19. Isaiah

The Book of Isaiah has always emerged preeminent among the Old Testament prophets for the Christian church. It is not surprising, therefore, to find numerous and rich writings on Isaiah, and any pastor's library without several good commentaries should be considered impoverished.

The modern historical critical method has left its strong impact on the literature. The most notable example is the dividing of the book between at least two different authors, the so-called First Isaiah and Second Isaiah. However, in my judgment, the basic issue is not touched by an immediate division into "conservative" and "liberal" camps. Rather, the search to distinguish good from bad exegesis cuts across the lines that are drawn to mark theological positions. Commentaries of excellent quality have been produced by scholars from both the left and the right. Conversely, both camps share the blame for much that is superficial and tedious. Because of the abundance of resources, I shall follow the procedure of first dealing with commentaries on the whole book, then those treating chs. 1 to 39, and finally those for chs. 40 to 66.

Commentaries on the entire book have the advantage of reflecting a unified perspective which is often missing when chapters are distributed among different commentators. However, it is understandable, because of the enormity of the task, that the practice of sharing the exegetical responsibility has dominated in recent years. Many of the commentaries on the entire book represent older works. In this category there are three classic commentaries that have long served the English-speaking world. I have in mind the volumes of Franz Delitzsch, John Skinner, and George Adam Smith. Delitzsch's famous commentary, which went through four editions, is a monument of immense learning, profound theological reflection, and sensitive literary interpretation. Of course, it is now old, and much of it is out-of-date, but the volume remains a classic which, in many respects, has not been replaced. However, the pastor should be warned that the commentary is not easy reading, but demands a serious and close study.

The solid, eminently reasonable commentary of John Skinner is very different from that of Delitzsch. It represents a much more critical literary approach, assigning the various chapters to a variety of different authors and periods. Also, the work is done with great caution and care. The volume is packed with information and provided with a mature exegetical judgment. Because of its condensed, somewhat dry style, the commentary, if used alone, might well frustrate the preacher. Fortunately, this omission is amply made up for by the vigorous commentary of George Adam Smith. One can object at many places to Smith's interpretation— I think he often circumvents the problem with a psychological ploy—yet one can still profit from his brilliant and lucid penetration into the prophetic message. In my opinion, Smith has sometimes captured a genuine canonical reading of the text even when claiming that his interpretation rested on fresh literary critical theory.

There is another very impressive two-volume commentary on the entire book by Edward J. Kissane. His commentary often is at odds with dominant critical theories; however, Kissane by no means simply represents a conservative reaction. He has offered a highly original and insightful approach which has continued to win supporters. Although his method is basically pre-form critical, only occasionally can he be faulted for being idiosyncratic.

Mention should be made of several other commentaries on the whole book. Bernhard Duhm's German commentary is one of the finest commentaries of this literary critical genre that has ever been written. Although its influence on English commentators has been widespread, no one else has been able to duplicate the brilliant literary analysis of this pioneer critic. The once widely used commentary of Thomas K. Cheyne has retained very little of value and can be easily bypassed. It is sad that this same judgment has to be made on Edward J. Young's *magnum opus.* Its highly polemical style and dogmatic categories have effectively blocked the author from getting close to the text. The contrast with Calvin's great commentary on Isaiah could hardly be greater. His Isaiah commentary is one of the Reformer's best and is full of lasting wisdom for those who know how to use it.

I am unenthusiastic about the several abbreviated modern commentaries on the book which are available. Of this type I suppose George Ernest Wright's commentary is the most useful.

If we now turn our attention to those commentaries which deal with the first half of the book, usually chs. 1 to 39, several modern treatments are available. Robert B. Y. Scott's contribution to *The Interpreter's Bible* is marked by its thorough and sensible approach and, in my judgment, ranks as one of the best in this series. Conversely, I have not found the standard volume of George B. Gray in the *International Critical Commentary* of much help. While sharing many of the radical features of Duhm's method, it lacks his brilliance and appears dull and mechanical. For the serious advanced student I would much prefer Otto Kaiser's more recent commentary. The two volumes, which cover chs. 1 to 39, differ widely in approach. His second volume is far more technical in character and illustrates the current trend toward redactional criticism. Neither have much to offer the pastor. Likewise, Hans Wildberger's ongoing commentary is of limited value to anyone not sharing a professional form critical interest. Of course, Walther Eichrodt's Isaiah commentary has a wide theological appeal, but its heavy style would hinder its popularity, even if it were to be translated into English. Finally, there are two brief English commentaries on chs. 1 to 39 by John Mauchline and Arthur S. Herbert, both of which are too elementary for the serious pastor.

Finally, an evaluation is in order for commentaries on chs. 40 to 66. The selection is quite overwhelming in number. James Muilenburg's introduction to the rhetorical features of the prophet's style remains classic. Yet I have found disappointment in being given an aesthetic judgment on a passage when a theological analysis is called for. Claus Westermann's more recent commentary is of high quality, but also quite one-sided in its focus. The constant attention to the formal features of prophetic oracles can be significant, of course, for serious exegesis, but it can also become an end in itself, to the pastor's enormous frustration. However, there is also a serious theological concern in Westermann, even if somewhat buried in this commentary. I would also tend to pass over the commentaries of Christopher R. North, John L. McKenzie, and R. Norman Whybray as duplicating material that can be found elsewhere. However, the French commentary of Pierre-E. Bonnard offers much fresh insight into both critical and theological issues.

There is another group of stimulating commentaries which, if used with discernment, can be of great profit. These commentaries share in common a highly speculative flavor which arises out of the need to provide so-called Deutero-Isaiah with a historical setting of some kind once the connection with First Isaiah had been severed. I have in mind the commentaries of Ulrich Simon, James D. Smart, and George A. F. Knight, all of whom in some degree reflect the influence of Charles C. Torrey. Simon's theological commentary is filled with profound and brilliant observations, but, because of its odd theories of composition, it has never had its proper impact. Likewise Smart's commentary has been dismissed as idiosyncratic because of its skeptical attitude toward the Cyrus passages. Still, Smart has some important insights into the eschatological function of the book. Knight's volume is far more attractive in its style and format than Smart's and represents a more standard approach to the critical questions. In my judgment, his book illustrates the difficulty of doing a theological analysis of a Biblical book when the canonical function has been replaced by the historical critical. However, all three of these volumes have something to offer.

Several monographs deserve mention in relation to chs. 40 to 66. The classic English study of the famous "servant songs" is by Christopher R. North and will profit the teacher more than the pastor. North's review of the various theories of interpretation of these important chapters is exceedingly well done. Actually an even more significant volume is that of Adolphe Neubauer and Samuel R. Driver, who have collected representative interpretations of Isa., ch. 53, by classic Jewish scholars. A study of this two-volume set can hardly be recommended to everyone, but a serious well-equipped student will uncover a wealth of unexpected treasure along with difficult theological issues.

I wish that I had better advice to give regarding good homiletical models in the use of Isaiah. Most of the sermons on Isaiah by the great church fathers (Chrysostom, Jerome, Theodoret) remain untranslated into English. Much of the traditional Protestant preaching is also highly allegorical and affords little attraction to the modern preacher. I would, however, mention Calvin's sermons as an exception not to be lightly dismissed. Karl Barth has also buried some highly provocative exegesis of Isaiah in the fine print of the *Church Dogmatics*.

20. Jeremiah

Of all the prophetic books of the Old Testament, the Book of Jeremiah is considered by many modern readers to be the most attractive. There appear to be several immediate accesses into the message of the book. It is particularly unfortunate, therefore, that good exegetical aids on this prophet are far from plentiful.

My first choice of a general commentary is John Bright's well-known volume in *The Anchor Bible*. This is the only recent full-scale commentary available. It is a solid, serious piece of exegesis and has served a generation well. However, the commentary has never been fully satisfactory, in my judgment. The attempt to force the book into a chronological scheme has resulted in constant rearrangment of passages. The exegetical emphasis falls on the historical data with far less attention to the literary shape of the book. Theological comments are surely present, but of a rather heavy-handed sort. Until something better appears, Bright remains at the top of the list.

The standard commentary in German is by Wilhelm Rudolph. It reflects great learning and meticulous attention to the text, yet I would not judge it to be one of his best contributions. For the teacher and the advanced student it offers a very useful tool until it is replaced. Several older German commentaries have played a large role in the history of scholarship, particularly in terms of literary and text criticism (e.g., Carl Heinrich Cornill, Bernhard Duhm, Paul Volz), but their commentaries are very dated and were never of immediate use to the pastor.

There are, however, several popular commentaries that can supplement Bright. The running debate between Stanley R. Hopper and James Philip Hyatt in *The Interpreter's Bible* offers some interesting perspectives on understanding Jeremiah. Ernest W. Nicholson has written a brief but thoroughly up-to-date commentary; however, for a reader who does not share Nicholson's critical theory of the role of the Deuteronomic editor in reshaping the original Jeremianic tradition, the exegesis will lose much of its value. Again, Roland K. Harrison's commentary presents the historical material of the book, but without any real exegetical skill.

Much more use could be made of some of the older commentaries. Arthur S. Peake's little commentary has long been regarded as one of the best contributions in the *Century Bible* series and can still be obtained inexpensively on the secondhand-book market. Leonard Elliott Binns's work also ranks as one of the better contributions in the *Westminster* series. The classic of this age is still George Adam Smith's *Jeremiah*. Although it never reached the heights of his commentary on the Minor Prophets, it is full of insight and stimulation for the homilist. In German, Artur Weiser and Helmut Lamparter have written good, popular commentaries which are also directed to the clergy.

I would also strongly recommend to the serious pastor, and certainly to the teacher, two excellent older monographs on Jeremiah. John Skinner's profound and thorough handling of the full range of issues in his *Prophecy and Religion* has gone a long way toward filling the gap left by the commentaries. Readily available in a paperback edition, it could well be used by an advanced adult class. The second monograph, by Adam C. Welch, is less lucid and balanced in judgment, but at times unsurpassed in its penetration. I prefer both these volumes to the "liberal" Jeremiah portrayed in the popular studies of Sheldon H. Blank and James Philip Hyatt.

There have always been many homiletical attempts to deal with Jeremiah, and some have left a genuine impact. Two very different approaches are represented by the studies of G. Campbell Morgan from the conservative camp and H. Wheeler Robinson from the liberal. Although there has always been a tendency among preachers to overpsychologize the portrait of Jeremiah, even this danger has testified eloquently to the enormous power of this book in the modern age.

21. Lamentations

The most useful, all-around commentary on Lamentations in English is Delbert R. Hillers' recent contribution to *The Anchor Bible*. The exegesis is mature, well balanced, and competent, touching on most of the major issues. Although the exposition is extremely cautious and sometimes lacking in excitement, the interpretation makes a valiant attempt to remain alert to the theological issues.

In addition, both pastor and teacher would do well to study Norman K. Gottwald's monograph on the theology of Lamentations. Indeed much of the credit for the contemporary interest on these issues goes to Gottwald for his creative attempt to interpret the book. In my judgment, Gottwald's thesis that the key to Lamentations lies in the tension between the Deuteronomic theology of reward and retribution and the historic reality cannot be sustained. Nevertheless, the book is stimulating and merits serious study.

There are three modern technical commentaries in German written by Hans-Joachim Kraus, Wilhelm Rudolph, and Otto Plöger. Kraus's treatment is a highly original, rather one-sided form critical study, which in the second edition has an important new section on the theology of Lamentations. Rudolph's very learned commentary expends much effort in determining the order in which the various poems were composed and offers some theological reflection in passing. Plöger offers a brief and highly condensed interpretation which seeks to delineate the various groups and religious traditions within the community of Palestine in the exilic period. Incidentally, the earlier edition by Max Haller in the same series is a very lively commentary more in the Gunkel tradition and should not be overlooked by the advanced student.

Of the older English commentaries Arthur S. Peake's is probably the most usable—his is certainly superior to Annesley W. Streane's—but it is not so full or theologically interesting as his commentary on Jeremiah.

Among the more recent homiletical commentaries mention first should be made of George A. F. Knight's strongly typological interpretation which pictures Lamentations speaking of the "crucifixion of God's adopted Son, Israel." Knight writes from a strongly confessional position, but his homiletical moves are creative and often powerful. It can be of great aid to the preacher if the interpretation is regarded as one theological actualization of the text among several other possibilities. Among the German commentaries of this genre, again Helmut Lamparter's is to be commended. Artur Weiser's is also useful but marred by his overemphasis on the cultic element.

22. Ezekiel

Remarkably rich exegetical resources are available in English on this difficult book. Walther Zimmerli's masterful commentary is scheduled shortly to appear in translation. It is hard to believe that this exhaustive commentary will be superseded within the next few generations. Not only does it provide all the technical research on text and philology but it excels in its detailed form critical analysis. Each section also concludes with a serious theological reflection. The major drawbacks of this commentary are its price and length. The prolix style calls for unusual fortitude on the part of the reader, yet the effort is rewarding. Certainly Zimmerli's commentary has replaced the earlier standard work of George A. Cooke, which was dull and theologically thin.

There are also two other good, modern commentaries available which supplement each other quite well. John W. Wevers' volume offers a precise, informative discussion of the major critical problems. It excels in the text critical issues, an area in which the author is outstanding. However, I have found the theological side of the commentary to be less impressive. There is a certain flatness—even sterility—in the exposition (cf. Ezek. 20:25; 37: 1–8) which will disappoint the pastor. Fortunately, the strengths and weaknesses of Walther Eichrodt's commentary are the reverse of those of Wevers'. The text critical work is minimal and Eichrodt's propensity to rearrange the canonical order appears often arbitrary and unilluminating. Eichrodt tends to have a heavy style, but he displays a profound theological grasp of the Old Testament which will reward the serious reader.

Particularly for the preacher some of the older commentaries remain of great value. I think that this quality stems from a theological understanding of the Old Testament which has not lost its vigorous connection either with the New Testament or with Christian theology. I value highly Andrew B. Davidson's classic old commentary in the *Cambridge Bible* because of its serious attempt to render the text's literal sense without getting lost in speculative theories. The commentary provides the kind of information needed by a pastor in brief compass. Carl F. Keil and Patrick Fairbairn reflect a good knowledge of the history of interpretation and discuss many theological issues that the modern commentator has dismissed. I prefer those two volumes to Ernst W. Hengstenberg, who is extremely learned but exceedingly tendentious. Personally I have found these mid-nineteenth century commentaries to be of more use than many volumes written at the turn of the century which are both thin and now out-of-date, such as Henry A. Redpath in the *Westminster* series. Also Herbert G. May's somewhat radical exegesis in *The Interpreter's Bible* has little to commend it.

There are some competent commentaries in German—I have in mind especially Johannes Herrmann and Georg Fohrer —but nothing that even closely rivals Zimmerli. By and large, the theological dimension of the text has been sorely neglected in favor of the literary and historical problems.

In my judgment, most of the more popular homiletical studies rest on a weak exegetical basis and can be safely bypassed. To my knowledge there is nothing in English that is as useful for sermon preparation as is the Swiss pastor Robert Brunner's practical commentary and Helmut Lamparter's *Zum Wächter bestellt*. However, Andrew W. Blackwood, Jr.'s, volume of expository sermons offers at least an attempt. Also Charles L. Feinberg's commentary is not to be disdained. His particular dispensationalist interpretation emerges mostly in the final section, but generally the volume is a lucid and practical study of the book, with some homiletical observations.

23. Daniel

The impact of the historical critical method on the Book of Daniel has been more dramatic than on most of the other books of the Old Testament. A sharp break came with the traditional understanding of Daniel when a new conclusion regarding its date of composition was accepted by a majority of scholars. Instead of the traditional sixth-century exilic period as the time of composition, the book was assigned to an unknown author of the Maccabean period. As a result, the usual method of introduction is to divide the commentaries into two groups according to whether they represent the traditional or the critical position. In my judgment, this move confuses an important issue. Good or poor exegesis cannot be determined on the basis of this one issue alone, but cuts across the conservative-critical syndrome. The fundamental task of exegesis—to determine what the literature means and how it functions as Scripture within the church— involves a host of interpretive skills shared in different degrees by commentators of both persuasions. I will, therefore, try to offer some reflected judgments on the level of excellence which is demonstrated among the various commentaries.

The most thorough commentary of all those in modern European languages in respect to questions of philology and text criticism is unquestionably that of the American scholar James A. Montgomery. With regard to the issues of the text, Montgomery has no close rival. There are, of course, other excellent philological commentaries, such as the older work of Anthony A. Bevan, but Montgomery is superior. Also the recent French commentary of Matthias Delcor has made an important contribution by its thorough research on the new textual material from Qumran.

From the conservative side Kenneth A. Kitchen's learned essay on problems of Aramaic is impressive too.

If we now turn to the larger questions of interpretation of the Book of Daniel, we find that the most influential commentary in English was Samuel R. Driver's lucid and closely argued volume of 1900. Driver did more than any other scholar to overcome the resistance to the critical position. Yet Driver's interpretation has flattened out the message of the book to make it a political tract for the Maccabean age from which the modern reader can extract, at most, a few lessons in piety. Theology has been transformed into anthropology. The same charge of politicizing the interpretation of Daniel can be made against the commentaries of Frederic W. Farrar, Robert H. Charles, and Arthur Jeffery. In a more sophisticated way, the two standard German commentaries by Aage Bentzen and Otto Plöger also use a reconstructed historical context to determine the content and function of the book.

Fortunately, two recent English commentaries by Eric W. Heaton and Norman W. Porteous, who are scholars of the critical position, have attempted to deal more seriously with the theological significance of Daniel. The strength of Heaton's vigorous commentary lies in its excellent introduction and consistent theological sensitivity. His actual exposition is less well developed because of the restricted space. Conversely, the contribution of Porteous' commentary lies in his mature exposition. Although no new critical literary solutions are offered, he often penetrates to the heart of the theological issue and sets the critical questions in a fresh light. His volume is certainly to be recommended to the serious pastor as a reliable guide.

From the conservative side, there are several older volumes that retain considerable value. Otto Zöckler offers one of the best reviews of the early history of interpretation available. Carl F. Keil's commentary is a model of enormous learning, although it contains far too many polemics. Edward J. Young is the modern counterpart to Keil. It may be his best commentary and is in a different scholarly class from the commentaries of John F. Walvoord or Robert D. Culver, in my opinion. Young's commentary is useful for its immense collection of material and knowledge of secondary literature. However, the actual handling of the Biblical text—for example, in its approach to narrative material—is deadening, to say the least. Perhaps good for lawyers, but not for preaching! In my judgment, the best modern commentary from a conservative stance is the German commentary of the great Catholic scholar Johann Goettsberger. He combines enormous learning with penetrating exegetical skills. His theology is creative and fresh.

There are many significant monographs on various subjects relating to Daniel and apocalyptic literature. I have never been enthusiastic about H. H. Rowley's *The Relevance of Apocalyptic,* but it has been widely used by teachers of the subject. I feel the same way about Klaus Koch's book on apocalyptic. In my judgment, two older books are far profounder in their grasp of the basic theological issues: Carl A. Auberlen's *The Prophecies of Daniel and the Revelation* (1856), and Adam C. Welch's *Visions of the End* (1922). Particularly Welch, through the experiences of World War I, catches a glimpse of the eschatological dimension of history.

For a homiletical guide, one is tempted to suggest the earliest Christian commentary still extant, that of Hippolytus, or the classic commentaries of Jerome and Calvin, but these are not easy to use without considerable prior training. My first choice would be the moving sermons of Walter Lüthi, now available in an English translation. Let it also be said that there is available a powerful example of how *not* to use Daniel in Hal Lindsey's all-too-familiar paperback, *The Late Great Planet Earth.*

24. The Minor Prophets

In the Hebrew canon the twelve small books of the prophets were linked together as one book to form a scroll approximately the same size as the three major prophets, Isaiah, Jeremiah, and Ezekiel. However, one of the great contributions of modern Old Testament scholarship has been the discovery of the striking individuality of each of the books and the enormous literary, historical, and theological richness of this collection. I propose treating first those commentaries which deal with the entire Book of the Twelve, and then discuss commentaries which treat individual books.

The English language has not been particularly rich in good commentaries that handle the entire collection of the Minor

Prophets. Because of great interest in these prophets, and also an early recognition of their complexity, modern English-speaking commentators have tended to focus on only one or two prophets. As a result, commentators on the whole collection usually represent an older period of scholarship.

The classic volume in English is unquestionably George Adam Smith's commentary on the Twelve. The pastor who is unacquainted with this volume has overlooked a remarkable resource. The strength of the book is in the brilliant style, keen perception, and theological seriousness with which the prophets were again brought to life. Of course, the exegesis is much out-of-date and reflects all the problems of the nineteenth-century literary critical approach. Moreover, the handling of the post-exilic prophets showed less insight than the earlier prophets. Nevertheless, this was a splendid achievement.

An even older set is the two-volume commentary of Carl F. Keil, which may well be his best commentary. Although it lacks the brilliance of Franz Delitzsch, Keil's great learning, sober scrutiny of the text, and awareness of the exegetical tradition of the church and the synagogue have made this a very useful volume. Keil's commentary serves as a good check on the romantic extravagencies of Smith. Only occasionally does Keil badly miss the plain sense of the text, as he does with the Book of Nahum.

There are several other older sets but they are of decidedly less value. One might have expected a rich diet of church fathers from Edward B. Pusey, but this is not the case. This exposition is apologetic, loosely philosophical, and without great value. Ebenezer Henderson's once highly prized commentary is mainly philological, and since this data is antiquated, the volume can be safely disregarded. I am somewhat more positive in my evaluation of the volume in the old J. P. Lange series, which includes many different authors. Each introduction sets out the history of exegesis with a thoroughness that is hard to find duplicated in more recent volumes. Particularly the Biblical books treated by Paul Kleinert are recommended.

The set of commentaries on the Minor Prophets in the *International Critical Commentary* presents a very mixed picture. The first volume, by William Rainey Harper, was a remarkable display of exhaustive scholarship on Amos and Hosea. In spite of this learning, the positions represented were so one-sided that the volume has lost most of its value. When Harper was unable to complete the rest of the Minor Prophets, the books were parceled out among four other scholars whose work was adequate but lacked both the learning and the thoroughness of Harper. Still, these latter volumes are better balanced than Harper's and furnish important technical information to the scholar. However, I would not place them high on a priority list for the pastor.

Turning next to foreign commentaries on the Minor Prophets, we find that there are several sets which deserve attention, particularly for the teacher and the advanced student of Old Testament. A superb volume from the older literary critical school has been written in French by Albin van Hoonacker. The exegesis is far richer than in the German commentaries of the same age, and grows in strength as it treats the post-exilic books. Another French set, which is very different in approach, appears in a modern French Protestant series and includes the contributions of such scholars as Carl A. Keller and Edmond Jacob. The commentary is comparable in its level to the German *Das Alte Testament Deutsch.* Like its German counterpart, some of the commentaries are more successful than others in addressing the needs of the pastor, but that is the avowed intent of the series. Most of the authors combine a modern form critical and historical approach with theological comments.

Among the German commentaries, Ernst Sellin's covers the entire Twelve in a very learned, but often highly arbitrary fashion which has reduced its value. A much-used commentary in the post-World War II period was by Theodore H. Robinson and Friedrich Horst, but the contributions, especially the first half by Robinson, were basically unsatisfactory. Horst's revision improved the level of critical scholarship, but did nothing to remove the theological sterility. The subsequent commentary of Artur Weiser and Karl Elliger attempted to improve on the situation, and certainly succeeded in some measure. Weiser's commentary on the first six books is richer in theology but weaker in exegetical insight. Elliger offers the reverse strengths, but in general his contribution has been more highly regarded. Certainly his critical analysis is far more original and creative. This general lack of good commentaries on the Twelve has called forth the efforts of both Hans Walter Wolff and Wilhelm Rudolph, whose individual commentaries will be discussed below.

There is a tremendous wealth of material for both pastor and teacher on the Book of Hosea. Hans Walter Wolff's recently translated commentary offers a highly detailed form critical study with an explicit concern to make his historical critical research bear theological fruit. Particularly for the advanced student the commentary provides a good avenue into a type of Old Testament scholarship which, under the leadership of von Rad, flourished in Germany after the post-war period. Space is too limited for an extensive criticism of Wolff's approach, but I am increasingly bothered by the fragile, speculative foundation on which much of the exegesis rests. In my judgment, Wolff's commentary, in spite of all its obvious strengths for which one is grateful, demonstrates the problem of trying to do justice to the theological dimension of a Biblical book without concern for its canonical shape. The strongest attack on Wolff from the critical side comes from Wilhelm Rudolph, whose thorough research on the older literary critical style focuses on Wolff's vulnerable points.

For the pastor I would recommend James L. Mays's commentary as my first choice, to be supplemented by the theological commentary of James M. Ward. Mays's exposition is specifically directed to the serious pastor. He has thus restricted himself to basic essentials, and provided a highly useful and practical exegetical resource. Mays's common sense has kept him from some of the extremes of Wolff's, but I would also fault his commentary for attempting to do his theological reflection on the basis of a theoretical reconstruction of the Biblical text rather than taking seriously its canonical function. Ward's commentary is recommended because of its extended theological reflection. Although I do not feel that the basic hermeneutical problem of Biblical exegesis is seen by him in more clarity, he has allowed himself much more space for a sustained and serious wrestling with the theological dimension of an Old Testament prophet, which will be greatly appreciated by the pastor. Of the older commentaries, Sydney L. Brown's contribution is still quite useful.

Mention should perhaps be made of the much-used brilliant homiletical study of H. Wheeler Robinson which first appeared under the title *The Cross of Hosea.* Unfortunately, his quasi-psychological category has turned the theology of Hosea completely on its head. In my judgment, it remains a classic cul-de-sac, to be used with discernment by those who learn best from failure.

Joel

Commentaries on this small book are frequently included with volumes on Amos. Hans Walter Wolff's commentary is surely the most complete in English, but once again, it should be checked by the sober scrutiny of Wilhelm Rudolph. Unfortunately, Rudolph's theological assessment of Joel is surprisingly negative. Douglas R. Jones has written a brief commentary, but for a succinct treatment I still prefer the tightly packed classic of Samuel R. Driver in the *Cambridge Bible*. As is true of most of Driver's works, his solid scholarship has endured the passing of time in a remarkable fashion.

Amos

Once again the reader is offered a rich and varied diet from which to choose. Hans Walter Wolff's commentary reflects similar strengths and weaknesses, and remains a great resource for the discerning student. Wilhelm Rudolph's equally learned German commentary plays a similar role in offering a very different interpretation of Amos. Again, my first choice of a commentary for the pastor would be James L. Mays's commentary. The careful exegesis and balanced judgment sets it in a different class from the more recent commentary by Ernst Hammershaimb, whose theological understanding leaves much to be desired. In my judgment, the older works of William Rainey Harper and Richard S. Cripps can be safely ignored, but I would still hold Samuel R. Driver's work in esteem.

For both pastor and teacher who seek to have Amos' message presented in a more systematic way, the monographs of John D. W. Watts and Arvid S. Kapelrud can probably be used with some profit, if the needed discernment is exercised.

Obadiah

Few individual commentaries have ever been written on this book. For the student a reliable, if undistinguished, manual is provided by John D. W. Watts. His cultic interpretation can be safely ignored.

Jonah

The Book of Jonah has continued to fascinate commentators. One of the best surveys of this history of interpretation can be found in Elias Bickerman's volume. For those who do not read Latin, Jerome's highly influential commentary is available in French and is a good representative of traditional Christian exegesis.

The traditional extremes in interpretation are still to be found. Gerhard Charles Aalders continues to rest the entire theological message of Jonah upon the complete historicity of the story, whereas Elias Bickerman dismisses such an approach as too obviously wrong even to discuss. For the advanced student the most thorough recent monograph is by Hans Walter Wolff, who treats the problems of extra-Biblical parallels, form critical issues, and theological significance with considerable skill. Rather recently two older conservative commentaries on Jonah, by Patrick Fairbairn and Hugh Martin, have been reprinted, but the heavily apologetic approach can hardly win much new support. For my part, I would recommend a very different sort of book to the pastor. Jacques Ellul's short monograph on Jonah is far more akin to the genre of sermon than commentary. Probably the book will satisfy neither the left nor the right in the traditional theological spectrum, but it represents a highly creative, robust theological interpretation which cannot but stimulate serious reflection.

Micah

For such an important book it is surprising to find so few serious commentaries. The announcement of James L. Mays's new commentary is therefore greatly welcomed. It will surely fill a serious gap in the field. The only possible rivals are the German commentary of Wilhelm Rudolph and the learned Dutch commentary of Adam S. van der Woude.

Nahum, Habakkuk, and Zephaniah

There is little choice in the study of these short books. The two older English commentaries by Andrew B. Davidson in the

Cambridge Bible and Samuel R. Driver in the *Century Bible* were always far too brief and are now out-of-date. Nevertheless, Davidson's volume retains considerable value for the pastor in its sober handling of the text with theological insight. John Eaton's volume in the *Torch Bible* is a generally reliable guide, but is very succinct. Walter A. Maier is the author of an extremely conservative, posthumously published commentary on Nahum. The interpretation of these three books by Rolf von Ungern-Sternberg and Helmut Lamparter is lively and attractive. Although the treatment of Nahum by Lamparter is quite brief, the exegesis is theologically rich.

Haggai, Zechariah, and Malachi

Of these three prophets, Zechariah has traditionally received by far the most attention. Much of the book's interest once derived from its frequent use by the New Testament. In more recent scholarship the renewed focus on apocalyptic literature has included the study of Zechariah. Numerous major monographs have appeared within the last decade, but no scholarly consensus has emerged and the discussion remains in great flux.

Unfortunately, most of the literature on Zechariah falls into two sharply distinguished camps. The older conservative commentaries, such as those by Charles H. H. Wright, David Baron, and Merrill Unger, have identified the New Testament's usage of Zechariah with the original intention of the prophet, and then they have tried to harmonize the two by means of a historical apologetic. The newer historical critical literature by such scholars as Kurt Galling, Paul D. Hanson, and others claims that the Book of Zechariah can be correctly interpreted only if the original historical setting is reconstructed, a dimension of the text which is notably missing in the present canonical form. One can only hope that this sterile hermeneutical impasse will be overcome by an interpretation that can hear the text as Scripture once again.

In my opinion, the best all-around commentary on these three prophets for the pastor is Joyce G. Baldwin's recent commentary. The approach of Baldwin is far more thorough and balanced than is the comparable volume of Douglas R. Jones. Baldwin's judgments are usually cautious, but she handles the critical questions in an honest fashion. I appreciate her attempt to distinguish between the question of the unity of original authorship and the integrity of the book in its canonical shape.

In conclusion, I would like to return to the issue of the homiletical use of the entire Book of the Twelve Minor Prophets. Several books are available that attempt in the brief compass of a chapter to catch the message of each prophet. The usefulness of such a book for a sermon series or an adult Bible class is evident. Unfortunately, most of the books of this type are badly out-of-date and distort each prophet by a crude reductionism. I suspect that George L. Robinson's book on the Twelve might still be a useful model if used with great discernment. The lucid outlines and serious attempt to meet the needs of the pastor are commendable. In spite of its many problems I greatly prefer it to Raymond Calkins' similar attempt.

Finally, I would put in a strong word for the classic commentaries of the Reformers as providing excellent models by which to learn the art of Biblical interpretation within the context of the worshiping community. Calvin's sermons on the Minor Prophets are published in five volumes. The same audience participation is everywhere evident in Luther's commentaries, and they continue to delight and surprise readers.

Abbreviations

AncB	The Anchor Bible
ATD	Das Alte Testament Deutsch
BAT	Botschaft des Alten Testaments
BKAT	Biblischer Kommentar: Altes Testament
CAT	Commentaires de L'Ancien Testament
CB	Cambridge Bible for Schools and Colleges
CeB	Century Bible
CNEB	Cambridge Bible Commentary on the New English Bible
ETB	Études Bibliques
ExB	The Expositor's Bible
ExHAT	Exegetisches Handbuch zum Alten Testament
HAT	Handbuch zum Alten Testament
Her	Hermeneia
HKAT	Göttinger Handkommentar zum Alten Testament
HSAT	Die Heilige Schrift des Alten Testaments
IB	The Interpreter's Bible
ICC	International Critical Commentary
KAT	Kommentar zum Alten Testament
KEH	Kurzgefasstes exegetisches Handbuch zum Alten Testament
KHC	Kurzer Hand-Commentar zum Alten Testament
LaBC	The Layman's Bible Commentary
LCHS	Johann Peter Lange (ed.), A Commentary on the Holy Scripture
LD	Lectio Divina
NCeB	New Century Bible
NICOT	The New International Commentary on the Old Testament
OTL	Old Testament Library
POT	De Prediking van het Oude Testament
SB	Sources Bibliques

TBC	Torch Bible Commentaries
TOTC	Tyndale Old Testament Commentaries
WC	Westminster Commentaries
ZB	Zürcher Bibelkommentare

Bibliography

Aalders, Gerhard Charles. *The Problem of the Book of Jonah.* London: Tyndale Press, 1948.

Ackroyd, Peter Runham. *The First Book of Samuel (CNEB).* Cambridge University Press, 1971.

———. *I and II Chronicles (TBC).* London: SCM Press, Ltd., 1973.

———. *Ezra, Nehemiah (TBC).* London: SCM Press, Ltd., 1973.

———. *Bible Bibliography 1967–1973. Old Testament.* Oxford: Basil Blackwell, 1974.

Adar, Zvi. *The Biblical Narrative.* Jerusalem: Department of Education and Cultures of the World Zionist Organization, 1959.

Aharoni, Yohanan. *The Land of the Bible: A Historical Geography.* Philadelphia: The Westminster Press, 1967.

Albright, William Foxwell. *The Archaeology of Palestine.* Middlesex, England: Penguin Books, Ltd., 1949.

Allen, Clifton J. (ed.). *The Broadman Bible Commentary.* Vols. I-VII. Nashville: The Broadman Press, 1969–1972.

Allmen, Jean Jacques von. *A Companion to the Bible.* London: Lutterworth Press, 1958.

Anderson, Arnold A. *Psalms (NCeB).* 2 vols. London: Oliphants, 1972.

Anderson, Bernhard Word. "The Book of Esther. Introduction and Exegesis," *The Interpreter's Bible,* Vol. III. Nashville: Abingdon Press, 1954. Pp. 821-874.

———. *Understanding the Old Testament.* Englewood Cliffs: Prentice-Hall, Inc., 1st ed. 1957; 3d ed. 1975.

Anderson, George Wishart (ed.). *A Decade of Bible Bibliography.* Oxford: Basil Blackwell, 1967.

Archer, Gleason Leonard, Jr. *A Survey of Old Testament Introduction.* Chicago: Moody Press, 1964.

Auberlen, Carl August. *The Prophecies of Daniel and the Revelation.* Edinburgh: T. & T. Clark, 1856.

Augustine, Saint. *Expositions on the Book of Psalms.* 6 vols. Oxford: John Henry Parker, 1847. Reprinted in abbrev. form by Wm. B. Eerdmans Publishing Company.

Baehr, Karl Christian W. F. *The Books of the Kings* (*LCHS*). Edinburgh: T. & T. Clark, 1872.

Baentsch, Bruno. *Exodus-Leviticus-Numeri (HKAT)*. Göttingen: Vandenhoeck & Ruprecht, 1903.

Baker, Joshua, and Nicholson, Ernest W. *The Commentary of Rabbi David Kimḥi on Psalms CXX-CL*. Cambridge University Press, 1973.

Baker, Richard. *Meditations and Disquisitions upon the First Psalm; the Penitential Psalms; and Seven Consolating Psalms*. 1639. Reprinted. London: Charles Higham, 1882.

Baldwin, Joyce G. *Haggai, Zechariah, Malachi (TOTC)*. London: Tyndale Press, 1972.

Ball, Charles J. *The Prophecies of Jeremiah (ExB)*. New York: Armstrong, 1890.

Barber, Cyril J. *The Minister's Library*. Grand Rapids: Baker Book House, 1974.

Bardtke, Hans. *Das Buch Esther (KAT)*. Gütersloh: Gütersloher Verlagshaus Gerd Mohn, 1963.

————. *Luther und das Buch Esther*. Tübingen: J. C. B. Mohr, 1964.

Barnes, William Emery. *The Two Books of Kings (CB)*. Rev. ed. Cambridge University Press, 1908.

————. *The Psalms (WC)*. 2 vols. London: Methuen & Co., Ltd., 1931.

————. *Haggai and Zechariah (CB)*. Rev. ed. Cambridge University Press, 1917.

Baron, David. *The Visions and Prophecies of Zechariah*. 1918. Reprinted. London: Marshall, Morgan and Scott, n.d.

Barr, James. *Old and New in Interpretation*. London: SCM Press, Ltd., 1966.

Barth, Christoph. *Introduction to the Psalms*. New York: Charles Scribner's Sons, 1966.

Barth, Karl. *Church Dogmatics*. Ed. and tr. by G. W. Bromiley and T. F. Torrance. 12 vols. Edinburgh: T. & T. Clark, 1936–1965.

Barton, George Aaron. *A Critical and Exegetical Commentary on the Book of Ecclesiastes (ICC)*. Edinburgh: T. & T. Clark, 1908.

Barucq, André. *Le Livre des Proverbes (SB)*. Paris: J. Gabalda, 1964.

Batten, Loring Woart. *A Critical and Exegetical Commentary on the Books of Ezra and Nehemiah (ICC)*. Edinburgh: T. & T. Clark, 1910.

Bauer, Johannes Baptist (ed.). *Encyclopedia of Biblical Theology*. 3 vols. London: Sheed & Ward, Ltd., 1970.

Begrich, Joachim. *Studien zu Deuterojesaja*. Stuttgart: Verlag W. Kohlhammer, 1938. Reprinted. Munich: Chr. Kaiser Verlag, 2d ed. 1969.

Bentzen, Aage. *Daniel (HAT)*. 2d ed. Tübingen: J. C. B. Mohr, 1952.

Bertheau, Ernst. *Die Bücher der Chronik (KEH)*. 2d ed. Leipzig: Verlag von S. Hirzel, 1873.

————. *Ezra und Nehemia (KEH)*. Leipzig: Verlag von S. Hirzel, 1862; 2d ed. 1887.

Bevan, Anthony Ashley. *A Short Commentary on the Book of Daniel*. Cambridge University Press, 1892.

Bickerman, Elias. *Four Strange Books of the Bible*. New York: Schocken Books, Inc., 1967.

Binns, Leonard Elliott. *The Book of Numbers (WC)*. London: Methuen & Co., Ltd., 1927.

————. *The Book of the Prophet Jeremiah (WC)*. London: Methuen & Co., Ltd., 1919.

Black, Matthew, and Rowley, Harold Henry (eds.). *Peake's Commentary on the Bible*. London: Thomas Nelson & Sons, 1962.

Blackwood, Andrew Watterson. *Preaching from Samuel*. New York: Abingdon-Cokesbury Press, 1946.

Blackwood, Andrew Watterson, Jr. *Ezekiel, Prophecy of Hope*. Grand Rapids: Baker Book House, 1965.

Blaikie, William Garden. *The Book of Joshua (ExB)*. New York: Armstrong, 1892.

————. *The First and Second Books of Samuel (ExB)*. New York: Armstrong, 1888.

Blank, Sheldon Haas. *Jeremiah—Man and Prophet*. Cincinnati: Hebrew Union College Press, 1961.

Boling, Robert G. *Judges (AncB)*. New York: Doubleday & Company, Inc., 1975.

Bonar, Andrew Alexander. *A Commentary on the Book of Leviticus*. London: James Nisbet, 1st ed. 1846; 4th ed. 1861.

Bonhoeffer, Dietrich. *Creation and Fall: A Theological Interpretation of Genesis 1-3*. New York: The Macmillan Company, 1959.

————. *Psalms: The Prayer Book of the Bible*. Minneapolis: Augsburg Publishing House, 1970.

Bonnard, Pierre-E. *Le Second Isaïe, son disciple et leurs éditeurs, Isa. 40-66 (ETB)*. Paris: J. Gabalda, 1972.

Bornkamm, Heinrich. *Luther and the Old Testament*. Philadelphia: Fortress Press, 1969.

Botterweck, G. Johannes, and Ringgren, Helmer (eds.). *Theological Dictionary of the Old Testament*. 2 vols. Grand Rapids: Wm. B. Eerdmans Publishing Company, 1974–1975.

Braude, William Gordon. *The Midrash on Psalms*. 2 vols. New Haven: Yale University Press, 1959.

Brenz, Johann. *Der Prediger Salomo*. 1528. Reprinted. Stuttgart: Friedrich Frommann Verlag, 1970.

Bridges, Charles. *An Exposition of the Book of Proverbs*. New York: Robert Carter, 1874. Reprinted. London: Banner of Truth.

Briggs, Charles Augustus. *A Critical and Exegetical Commentary on the Book of Psalms (ICC).* 2 vols. Edinburgh: T. & T. Clark, 1906.

Bright, John. *A History of Israel.* 2d ed. Philadelphia: The Westminster Press, 1972.

———. "The Book of Joshua. Introduction and Exegesis," *The Interpreter's Bible,* Vol. II. Nashville: Abingdon Press, 1953. Pp. 541–550, 553–673.

———. *Jeremiah (AncB).* New York: Doubleday & Company, Inc., 1965.

Brockington, Leonard H. *Ezra, Nehemiah and Esther (NCeB).* London: Thomas Nelson & Sons, 1969.

Brown, Francis; Driver, Samuel Rolles; Briggs, Charles A. *A Hebrew and English Lexicon of the Old Testament.* Oxford: Clarendon Press, 1907.

Brown, Raymond E.; Fitzmyer, Joseph A.; Murphy, Roland E. *The Jerome Biblical Commentary.* Englewood Cliffs: Prentice-Hall, Inc., 1968.

Brown, Sydney L. *The Book of Hosea (WC).* London: Methuen & Co., Ltd., 1932.

Brunner, Robert. *Ezekiel (ZB).* 2 vols. Zurich: Zwingli Verlag, 1st ed. 1944; 2d ed. 1969.

Buber, Martin. *The Kinship of God.* New York: Harper & Row, Publishers, Inc., 1967.

———. *Moses.* Oxford and London: East and West Library, 1946.

———. *The Prophetic Faith.* New York: The Macmillan Company, 1949.

Budde, Karl. *Das Hohelied (KHC).* Tübingen: J. C. B. Mohr, 1898.

———. *Die Bücher Samuel (KHC).* Tübingen: J. C. B. Mohr, 1902.

Buis, Pierre, and Leclercq, Jacques. *Le Deutéronome (SB).* Paris: J. Gabalda, 1963.

Burney, Charles Fox. *The Book of Judges.* 2d ed. London: Rivington, 1920. Reprinted. New York: Ktav Publishing House, Inc., 1966.

———. *Notes on the Hebrew Text of the Books of Kings.* Oxford: Clarendon Press, 1903. Reprinted. New York: Ktav Publishing House, Inc., 1966.

Burrowes, George. *A Commentary on the Song of Solomon.* Philadelphia: W. S. Martien, 1853. Reprinted. London: Banner of Truth.

Buttrick, George Arthur (ed.). *The Interpreter's Dictionary of the Bible.* 4 vols. Nashville: Abingdon Press, 1962.

Buzy, Denis. *Le Cantique des Cantiques.* Paris: Letouzey et Ané, 1949.

Caird, George Bradford. "The First and Second Books of Samuel. Introduction and Exegesis," *The Interpreter's Bible,* Vol. II. Nashville: Abingdon Press, 1953. Pp. 855–1176.

Calkins, Raymond. *The Modern Message of the Minor Prophets.* New York: Harper & Brothers, 1947.

Calmet, Augustin. *Bibliotheca Sacra. A Historical, Critical, Geographical, and Etymological Dictionary of the Bible.* Vol. III. Folio edition. London, 1732.

Calvin, John. *Sermons upon the fifth booke of Moses, called Deuteronomie.* Folio. London, 1584.

————. *Sermons from Job.* Grand Rapids: Wm. B. Eerdmans Publishing Company, 1952.

————. *The Gospel According to Isaiah. Seven Sermons on Isa. 53.* Grand Rapids: Wm. B. Eerdmans Publishing Company, 1953.

————. *The Works of John Calvin.* Edinburgh: Calvin Translation Society, 1843–1855. Reprinted. T. & T. Clark and Wm. B. Eerdmans Publishing Company.

Campbell, Edward F., Jr. *Ruth (AncB).* New York: Doubleday & Company, Inc., 1975.

Campbell, Edward F., Jr.; Freedman, David Noel; Wright, George Ernest (eds.). *The Biblical Archaeologist Reader.* 3 vols. New York: Doubleday & Company, Inc. 1961–1970.

Cassuto, Umberto. *Commentary on the Book of Genesis.* Vol. I: *From Adam to Noah;* Vol II: *Noah to Abraham.* Jerusalem: Magnes Press, 1961–1964.

————. *A Commentary on the Book of Exodus.* Jerusalem: Magnes Press, 1967.

Cave, Alfred. *An Introduction to Theology.* 2d ed. Edinburgh: T. & T. Clark, 1896.

Chadwick, George A. *The Book of Exodus (ExB).* New York: Armstrong, 1890.

Chapman, Arthur T., and Streane, Annesley William. *The Book of Leviticus (CB).* Rev. ed. Cambridge University Press, 1914.

Charles, Robert Henry. *A Critical and Exegetical Commentary on the Book of Daniel.* Oxford: Clarendon Press, 1929.

Cheyne, Thomas Kelly. *The Prophecies of Isaiah.* 2 vols. London: Kegan Paul, 1st ed. 1880; 3d ed. 1886.

————. *The Book of Hosea (CB).* Cambridge University Press, 1913.

————. *Micah (CB).* Cambridge University Press, 1882.

————, and Black, John Sutherland (eds.). *Encyclopaedia Biblica.* 4 vols. New York: The Macmillan Company, 1899–1903.

Childs, Brevard Springs. *The Book of Exodus (OTL).* Philadelphia: The Westminster Press, 1974.

Clarke, Adam. *The Holy Bible containing the Old and New Testaments with a Commentary and Critical Notes.* 6 vols. London: W. Tegg, 1844. Reprinted. Abingdon-Cokesbury Press.

Clements, Ronald E. *Exodus (CNEB).* Cambridge University Press, 1972.

————. *God's Chosen People.* London: SCM Press, Ltd., 1968.

Cole, Robert Allan. *Exodus (TOTC).* London: Inter-Varsity Press, 1973.

Cooke, George Albert. *The Book of Joshua (CB).* Rev. ed. Cambridge University Press, 1918.

_____. *The Book of Judges (CB)*. Rev. ed. Cambridge University Press, 1913.

_____. *The Book of Ruth (CB)*. Rev. ed. Cambridge University Press, 1918.

_____. *A Critical and Exegetical Commentary on the Book of Ezekiel (ICC)*. Edinburgh: T. & T. Clark, 1937.

Cornill, Carl Heinrich. *Das Buch Jeremia erklärt*. Leipzig: C. H. Tauchnitz, 1905.

Cowley, Arthur E. *Gesenius' Hebrew Grammar as edited and enlarged by Emil Kautzsch*. 28th ed. Oxford: Clarendon Press, 1910.

Cox, Samuel. *Commentary on the Book of Job*. London: C. Kegan Paul and Co., 1880.

_____. *The Book of Ecclesiastes (ExB)*. New York: Armstrong, 1890.

Craigie, Peter C. *The Book of Deuteronomy (NICOT)*. Grand Rapids: Wm. B. Eerdmans Publishing Company, 1976.

Cripps, Richard Seymour. *A Critical and Exegetical Commentary on the Book of Amos*. 2d ed. London: S.P.C.K., 1955.

Cruden, Alexander. *A Complete Concordance to the Holy Scriptures*. New York: Dodd and Mead, 1870.

Culver, Robert Duncan. *Daniel and the Latter Days*. Chicago: Moody Press, 1954.

Cundall, Arthur E. *Judges (TOTC)*. London: Tyndale Press, 1968.

Cunliffe-Jones, Hubert. *Deuteronomy (TBC)*. London: SCM Press, Ltd., 1951.

_____. *Jeremiah (TBC)*. London: SCM Press, Ltd., 1960.

Curtis, Edward Lewis, and Madsen, Albert Alonzo. *A Critical and Exegetical Commentary on the Books of Chronicles (ICC)*. Edinburgh: T. & T. Clark, 1910.

Dahood, Mitchell. *Psalms (AncB)*. 3 vols. New York: Doubleday & Company, Inc., 1966–1970.

Danker, Frederick W. *Multipurpose Tools for Bible Study*. 3d ed. St. Louis: Concordia Publishing House, 1970.

Darling, James. *Cyclopaedia Bibliographia: A Library Manual for Authors, Preachers, Students, and Literary Men*. 2 vols. London: James Darling, 1854.

Davidson, Andrew Bruce. *The Book of Job (CB)*. Cambridge University Press, 1884.

_____. *The Book of the Prophet Ezekiel (CB)*. Rev. ed. Cambridge University Press, 1916.

_____. *The Books of Nahum, Habakkuk and Zephaniah (CB)*. Cambridge University Press, 1896.

_____. *The Theology of the Old Testament*. Edinburgh: T. & T. Clark, 1904.

Davidson, Robert. *Genesis I-XI (CNEB)*. Cambridge University Press, 1963.

Davies, Gwynne Henton. *Exodus: Introduction and Commentary (TBC)*. London: SCM Press, Ltd., 1967.

Deissler, Alfons. *Die Psalmen*. 3 vols. Düsseldorf: Patmos-Verlag, 1963.

Delcor, Matthias. *Le Livre de Daniel (SB)*. Paris: J. Gabalda, 1971.

Delitzsch, Franz. *A New Commentary on Genesis*. 2 vols. 5th ed. Edinburgh: T. & T. Clark, 1899.

————. *Biblical Commentary on the Book of Job*. 2 vols. 2d ed. Edinburgh: T. & T. Clark, 1872.

————. *Biblical Commentary on the Psalms*. 3 vols. 2d ed. Edinburgh: T. & T. Clark, 1871.

————. *Biblical Commentary on the Proverbs of Solomon*. 2 vols. Edinburgh: T. & T. Clark, 1874–1875.

————. *Biblical Commentary on the Song of Songs and Ecclesiastes*. Edinburgh: T. & T. Clark, 1877.

————. *Biblical Commentary on the Prophecies of Isaiah*. 2 vols. 4th ed. Edinburgh: T. & T. Clark, 1894.

Dhorme, Edouard. *A Commentary on the Book of Job*. London: Thomas Nelson & Sons, 1967.

Dickson, David. *A Commentary on the Psalms*. 1653–1655. Reprinted. London: Banner of Truth, 1957.

Dillmann, August. *Genesis: Critically and Exegetically Expounded*. 2 vols. Edinburgh: T. & T. Clark, 1897.

————. *Die Bücher Numeri, Deuteronomium und Joshua (KEH)*. Leipzig: Verlag von S. Hirzel, 1886.

Dods, Marcus. *The Book of Genesis (ExB)*. New York: Armstrong, 1893.

Dommershausen, Werner. *Die Estherrolle*. Stuttgart: Verlag Katholisches Bibelwerk, 1968.

Donne, John. *Sermons on the Psalms and Gospels*. Berkeley: University of California Press, 1963.

Drijvers, Pius. *The Psalms: Their Structure and Meaning*. New York: Herder & Herder, Inc., 1965.

Driver, Samuel Rolles. *The Book of Genesis (WC)*. London: Methuen & Co., Ltd., 1904.

————. *The Book of Exodus (CB)*. Cambridge University Press, 1911.

————. *A Critical and Exegetical Commentary on Deuteronomy (ICC)*. Edinburgh: T. & T. Clark, 1895.

————. *Notes on the Hebrew Text and Typography of the Books of Samuel*. Oxford: Clarendon Press, 1913.

————, and Gray, George Buchanan. *A Critical and Exegetical Commentary on the Book of Job (ICC)*. 2 vols. Edinburgh: T. & T. Clark, 1921.

————. *The Book of Daniel (CB)*. Cambridge University Press, 1900.

_____. *The Books of Joel and Amos (CB)*. Rev. ed. Cambridge University Press, 1915.

_____. *The Minor Prophets. Nahum, Habakkuk, Zephaniah, Haggai, Zechariah, Malachi (CeB)*. London: Nelson and Sons, 1906.

Duhm, Bernhard. *Das Buch Jesaia, übersetzt und erklärt (HKAT)*. 4th ed. Göttingen: Vandenhoeck & Ruprecht, 1922.

_____. *Das Buch Jeremia (KHC)*. Tübingen: J. C. B. Mohr, 1901.

Eaton, John H. *Obadiah, Nahum, Habakkuk and Zephaniah (TBC)*. London: SCM Press, Ltd., 1961.

Eichrodt, Walther. *Der Heilige in Israel. Jesaja 1–12; Der Herr der Geschichte. Jesaja 13–23, 28–39 (BAT)*. 2 vols. Stuttgart: Calwer Verlag 1960–1967.

_____. *Ezekiel (OTL)*. Philadelphia: The Westminster Press, 1970.

_____. *Theology of the Old Testament (OTL)*. 2 vols. Philadelphia: The Westminster Press, 1961,1967.

Eissfeldt, Otto. *The Old Testament: An Introduction*. New York: Harper & Row, Publishers, Inc., 1965.

Elliger, Karl. *Leviticus (HAT)*. Tübingen: J. C. B. Mohr, 1966.

_____. *Jesaja II (BKAT)*. Neukirchen-Vluyn: Neukirchener Verlag, 1973–.

Ellison, Henry Leopold. *Ezekiel: The Man and His Message*. Grand Rapids: Wm. B. Eerdmans Publishing Company, 1956.

Ellison, John William (comp.). *Nelson's Complete Concordance of the Revised Standard Version Bible*. New York: Thomas Nelson & Sons, 1957.

Ellul, Jacques. *The Judgment of Jonah*. Grand Rapids: Wm. B. Eerdmans Publishing Company, 1971.

_____. *The Politics of God and the Politics of Man*. Grand Rapids: Wm. B. Eerdmans Publishing Company, 1972.

Elmslie, William Alexander Leslie. *The Book of Chronicles (CB)*. Cambridge University Press, 1916.

Fairbairn, Patrick. *An Exposition of Ezekiel*. Edinburgh: T. & T. Clark, 1851. Reprinted. Grand Rapids: Sovereign Grace Publishers, 1971.

_____. *Jonah. His Life, Character, and Mission*. Edinburgh: Johnstone, 1849. Reprinted. Grand Rapids: Kregel Publications, 1964.

Farrar, Frederic William. *The First and Second Books of Kings (ExB)*. 2 vols. New York: Armstrong, 1892–1893.

_____. *The Book of Daniel (ExB)*. New York: Armstrong, 1903.

Feinberg, Charles Lee. *The Prophecy of Ezekiel*. Chicago: Moody Press, 1969.

Feuillet, André. *Le Cantique des Cantiques (LD)*. Paris: Éditions du Cerf, 1953.

Fichtner, Johannes. *Das erste Buch von den Königen (BAT)*. Stuttgart: Calwer Verlag, 1964.

Fohrer, Georg. *Das Buch Hiob (KAT)*. Gütersloh: Gütersloher Verlagshaus Gerd Mohn, 1963.

———. *Ezechiel (HAT)*. 2d ed. Tübingen: J. C. B. Mohr, 1955.

———. *Introduction to the Old Testament*. Nashville: Abingdon Press, 1968.

Frei, Hans. *The Eclipse of Biblical Narrative*. New Haven: Yale University Press, 1974.

Fricke, Klaus Dietrich. *Das zweite Buch von den Königen (BAT)*. Stuttgart: Calwer Verlag, 1972.

Fuller, Andrew. *Expository Discourses on the Book of Genesis. Works*, Vol. V. New York: S. Converse, 1825.

Galling, Kurt. *Die Bücher der Chronik, Ezra, Nehemia (ATD)*. Göttingen: Vandenhoeck & Ruprecht, 1954.

———. *Der Prediger. Die fünf Megilloth (HAT)*. Tübingen: J. C. B. Mohr, 1969.

——— (ed.). *Die Religion in Geschichte und Gegenwart*. 3d ed. Tübingen: J. C. B. Mohr, 1957–1965.

Garstang, John. *Joshua, Judges*. London: Constable & Co., Ltd., 1931.

Gehman, Henry Snyder (ed.). *The New Westminster Dictionary of the Bible*. Philadelphia: The Westminster Press, 1970.

Gemser, Berend. *Sprüche Salomos (HAT)*. 2d ed. Tübingen: J. C. B. Mohr, 1963.

Gerleman, Gillis. *Esther (BKAT)*. Neukirchen-Vluyn: Neukirchener Verlag, 1960.

———. *Ruth. Das Hohelied (BKAT)*. Neukirchen-Vluyn: Neukirchener Verlag, 1965.

Gibson, Edgar C. S. *The Book of Job (WC)*. London: Methuen & Co., Ltd., 1919.

Gill, John. *An Exposition of the Song of Solomon*. London, 1728. Reprinted. Grand Rapids: Sovereign Grace Publishers, 1971.

Ginsburg, Christian David. *Coheleth and Song of Songs*. 2 vols. 1857–1861. Reprinted. New York: Ktav Publishing House, Inc., 1970.

Glanzman, George S. *An Introductory Bibliography for the Study of Scripture*. Westminster, Md.: The Newman Press, 1961.

Glatzer, Nahum N. *The Dimensions of Job: A Study and Selected Readings*. New York: Schocken Books, Inc., 1969.

Goettsberger, Johann. *Die Bücher der Chronik oder Paralipomenon (HSAT)*. Bonn: Peter Hanstein, 1939.

———. *Das Buch Daniel (HSAT)*. Bonn: Peter Hanstein, 1928.

Gordis, Robert. *Koheleth: The Man and His World*. New York: Jewish Theological Seminary of America, 1951. Reprinted. Schocken Books, Inc., 1968.

_____. *The Song of Songs and Lamentations.* Rev. ed. New York: Ktav Publishing House, Inc., 1974.

Gore, Charles; Goudge, Henry Leighton; Guillaume, Alfred (eds.). *A New Commentary on Holy Scripture Including the Apocrypha.* London: S.P.C.K., 1928.

Gottwald, Norman Karol. *A Light to the Nations: An Introduction to the Old Testament.* New York: Harper & Row, Publishers, Inc., 1959.

_____. *Studies in the Book of Lamentations.* London: SCM Press, Ltd., 1959.

Gray, George Buchanan. *A Critical and Exegetical Commentary on the Book of Numbers (ICC).* Edinburgh: T. & T. Clark, 1903.

_____. *A Critical and Exegetical Commentary on the Book of Isaiah, Chs. 1–27 (ICC).* Edinburgh: T. & T. Clark, 1912.

Gray, John. *Joshua, Judges, and Ruth (NCeB).* London: Thomas Nelson & Sons, 1967.

_____. *I and II Kings (OTL).* 2d ed. Philadelphia: The Westminster Press, 1971.

Greenslade, Stanley Lawrence; Lampe, Geoffrey William Hugo; Ackroyd, Peter Runham (eds.). *The Cambridge History of the Bible.* 3 vols. Cambridge University Press, 1963–1970.

Gregory the Great. *On the Book of Job (Magna Moralia).* 4 vols. London: James Parker, 1844–1850.

Gressmann, Hugo. *Mose und seine Zeit.* Göttingen: Vandenhoeck & Ruprecht, 1913.

Gros Louis, Kenneth R. R., and others (eds.). *Literary Interpretations of Biblical Narratives.* Nashville: Abingdon Press, 1974.

Gunkel, Hermann. *Genesis (HKAT).* 4th ed. Göttingen: Vandenhoeck & Ruprecht, 1917.

_____. *Esther.* Tübingen: J. C. B. Mohr, 1916.

_____. *Die Psalmen (HKAT).* Göttingen: Vandenhoeck & Ruprecht, 1926.

_____. *The Psalms (Facet Books).* Philadelphia: Fortress Press, 1967.

Gutbrod, Karl. *Das Buch vom König: Das erste Buch Samuel; Das Buch vom Reich: Das zweite Buch Samuel (BAT).* 2 vols. Stuttgart: Calwer Verlag, 1956–1958.

Guthrie, Donald; Motyer, J. Alec; Stibbs, Alan M.; Wiseman, Donald John (eds.). *The New Bible Commentary.* London: Inter-Varsity Press, 1970.

Haller, Max. *Die fünf Megilloth (HAT).* Tübingen: J. C. B. Mohr, 1940.

Hals, Ronald M. *The Theology of the Book of Ruth (Facet Books).* Philadelphia: Fortress Press, 1966.

Hammershaimb, Ernst. *The Book of Amos.* Oxford: Basil Blackwell, 1970.

Hanson, Paul D. *The Dawn of Apocalyptic.* Philadelphia: Fortress Press, 1975.

Harper, Andrew. *The Song of Solomon (CB)*. Cambridge University Press, 1912.

Harper, William Rainey. *A Critical and Exegetical Commentary on the Books of Amos and Hosea (ICC)*. Edinburgh: T. & T. Clark, 1905.

Harrison, Roland Kenneth. *Introduction to the Old Testament*. Grand Rapids: Wm. B. Eerdmans Publishing Company, 1969.

———. *Jeremiah and Lamentations: An Introduction and Commentary (TOTC)*. London: Tyndale Press, 1973.

Hastings, James (ed.). *A Dictionary of the Bible*. 5 vols. New York: Charles Scribner's, 1901–1904.

———. *Encyclopaedia of Religion and Ethics*. 13 vols. New York: Charles Scribner's, 1908–1912.

Heaton, Eric William. *The Book of Daniel (TBC)*. London: SCM Press, Ltd., 1956.

Henderson, Ebenezer. *The Book of the Twelve Minor Prophets*. Andover: W. I. Draper, 1868.

Hengstenberg, Ernst Wilhelm. *Commentary on the Psalms*. 3 vols. Edinburgh: T. & T. Clark, 1851.

———. *Commentary on Ecclesiastes*. Edinburgh: T. & T. Clark, 1860.

———. *The Prophecies of the Prophet Ezekiel Elucidated*. Edinburgh: T. & T. Clark, 1869.

Henry, Matthew. *An Exposition of the Old and New Testament*. 6 vols. Philadelphia: Towar and Hogan, 1828. Frequently reprinted.

Herbert, Arthur Summer. *Genesis 12–50 (TBC)*. London: SCM Press, Ltd., 1962.

———. *The Book of the Prophet Isaiah, Chs. 1–39 (CNEB)*. Cambridge University Press, 1973.

Herder, Johann Gottfried von. *The Spirit of Hebrew Poetry*. 2 vols. 1782–1783. Burlington: Edward Smith, 1833. Reprinted. Alec R. Allenson, Inc.

Herrmann, Johannes. *Ezechiel (KAT)*. Leipzig: Deichert, 1924.

Herrmann, Siegfried. *A History of Israel in Old Testament Times*. Philadelphia: Fortress Press, 1973.

Hertzberg, Hans Wilhelm. *Die Bücher Joshua, Richter, Ruth (ATD)*. Göttingen: Vandenhoeck & Ruprecht, 1953.

———. *I and II Samuel (OTL)*. Philadelphia: The Westminster Press, 1965.

———. *Der Prediger (KAT)*. 2d ed. Gütersloh: Gütersloher Verlagshaus Gerd Mohn, 1963.

Hillers, Delbert R. *Lamentations (AncB)*. New York: Doubleday & Company, Inc., 1972.

Hippolyte. *Commentaire sur Daniel (SC)*. Paris: Éditions du Cerf, 1947.

Hölscher, Gustav. *Das Buch Hiob (HAT)*. 2d ed. Tübingen: J. C. B. Mohr, 1952.

Hoffmann, David. *Das Buch Leviticus.* 2 vols. Berlin: M. Poppelauer Verlag, 1905–1906.

Holladay, William Lee. *A Concise Hebrew and Aramaic Lexicon of the Old Testament.* Leiden: E. J. Brill, 1971.

Hoonacker, Albin van. *Les Douze Petits Prophètes (ETB).* Paris: J. Gabalda, 1908.

Horne, Thomas Hartwell. *An Introduction to the Critical Study and Knowledge of the Holy Scriptures.* Vol. V. 9th ed. London: Longman, Brown, Green and Longmans, 1846.

Horton, Robert Forman. *The Minor Prophets. Hosea, Joel, Amos, Obadiah, Jonah, and Micah (CeB).* Edinburgh: T. C. & E. C. Jack, n.d.

Hyatt, James Philip. *Exodus (NCeB).* London: Oliphants, 1971.

———, and Hopper, Stanley Romaine. "The Book of Jeremiah," *The Interpreter's Bible,* Vol. V. Nashville: Abingdon Press, 1956. Pp. 775–1142.

———. *Jeremiah, Prophet of Courage and Hope.* Nashville: Abingdon Press, 1958.

Jacob, Benno. *Das erste Buch der Tora. Genesis.* 1934. Reprinted. Ktav Publishing House, Inc., 1974.

Jacob, Edmond. *Theology of the Old Testament.* New York: Harper & Brothers, 1958.

———; Amsler, S.; Keller, C. A. *Les Petits Prophètes: Osée, Joël, Amos, Abdias, Jonas (CAT).* Neuchâtel: Delachaux & Niestlé, 1965.

James, Fleming. *Personalities of the Old Testament.* New York: Charles Scribner's Sons, 1939.

Jeffery, Arthur. "The Book of Daniel. Introduction and Exegesis," *The Interpreter's Bible,* Vol. VI. Nashville: Abingdon Press, 1956. Pp. 341–354, 359–549.

Jerome, Saint. *The Homilies of Saint Jerome on the Psalms (The Fathers of the Church),* Vols. 48, 57). Washington, D.C.: The Catholic University of America Press, 1964, 1966.

———. *Jerome's Commentary on Daniel.* Tr. by G. L. Archer. Grand Rapids: Baker Book House, 1958.

———. *Sur Jonas (SC).* Paris: Éditions du Cerf, 1956.

Jones, Douglas Rawlinson. *Isaiah 56–66 and Joel (TBC).* London: SCM Press, Ltd., 1964.

———. *Haggai, Zechariah, and Malachi (TBC).* London: SCM Press, Ltd., 1962.

Joüon, Paul. *Ruth. Commentaire philologique et exégétique.* Rome: Institut Biblique Pontifical, 1953.

Jung, Carl Gustaf. *Answer to Job.* London: R. F. C. Hull, 1954.

Kaiser, Otto. *Introduction to the Old Testament.* Oxford: Basil Blackwell, 1975.

102

————. *Isaiah 1–12; Isaiah 13–39 (OTL)*. 2 vols. Philadelphia: The Westminster Press, 1972, 1974.

Kalisch, Marcus Moritz. *A Historical and Critical Commentary on the Old Testament: Genesis*. London: Longman, Brown, Green and Longmans, 1858.

————. *A Historical and Critical Commentary on the Old Testament: Exodus*. London: Longman, Brown, Green and Longmans, 1855.

Kapelrud, Arvid Schou. *Central Ideas in Amos*. 2d ed. Oslo: Oslo University Press, 1961.

Keil, Carl Friedrich. *Biblical Commentary on the Pentateuch*. 3 vols. Edinburgh: T. & T. Clark, 1864–1865. Entire series reprinted by Wm. B. Eerdmans Publishing Company.

————. *Biblical Commentary on the Books of Joshua, Judges, Ruth*. Edinburgh: T. & T. Clark, 1868.

————. *Biblical Commentary on the Books of Samuel*. 2d ed. Edinburgh: T. & T. Clark, 1875.

————. *Biblical Commentary on the Books of the Kings*. 2d ed. Edinburgh: T. & T. Clark, 1876.

————. *Biblical Commentary on the Books of the Chronicles*. Edinburgh: T. & T. Clark, 1872.

————. *Biblical Commentary on the Books of Ezra, Nehemiah, and Esther*. Edinburgh: T. & T. Clark, 1888.

————. *Biblical Commentary on the Prophecies of Jeremiah*. 2 vols. Edinburgh: T. & T. Clark, 1880.

————. *Biblical Commentary on the Book of Ezekiel*. 2 vols. Edinburgh: T. & T. Clark, 1882.

————. *Biblical Commentary on the Book of the Prophet Daniel*. Edinburgh: T. & T. Clark, 1872.

————. *Biblical Commentary on the Twelve Minor Prophets*. 2 vols. Edinburgh: T. & T. Clark, 1868.

Keller, Carl A., and Vuilleumier, René. *Les Petits Prophètes: Michée, Nahoum, Habacuc, Soponie (CAT)*. Neuchâtel: Delachaux et Niestlé, 1971.

Kennedy, Archibald Robert Sterling. *Leviticus and Numbers (CeB)*. Edinburgh: T. C. & E. C. Jack, n.d.

————. *Samuel (CeB)*. Edinburgh: T. C. & E. C. Jack, 1905.

Kidner, Derek. *Genesis. An Introduction and a Commentary (TOTC)*. London: Tyndale Press, 1967.

————. *The Proverbs (TOTC)*. London: Tyndale Press, 1964.

Kimḥi, Rabbi. *The Commentary of Rabbi David Kimḥi on Psalms CXX–CL*. Translation and Glossary by Ernest W. Nicholson and Joshua Baker. Cambridge University Press, 1973.

Kirkpatrick, Alexander Francis. *The First and Second Book of Samuel (CB)*. Cambridge University Press, 1st ed. 1881; 2d ed. 1930.

_____. *The Book of Psalms (CB)*. 3 vols. Cambridge University Press, 1910.

Kissane, Edward Joseph. *The Book of Psalms*. 2 vols. Dublin: Browne & Nolan, Ltd., 1952–1954.

_____. *The Book of Isaiah*. 2 vols. Dublin: Browne & Nolan, Ltd., 1941–1944.

Kitchen, Kenneth Anderson, with Wiseman, Donald John *et al. Notes on Some Problems in the Book of Daniel*. London: Tyndale Press, 1965.

Kittel, Gerhard, and Friedrich, Gerhard. *Theological Dictionary of the New Testament*. 9 vols. Grand Rapids: Wm. B. Eerdmans Publishing Company, 1964–1973.

Kittel, Rudolf. *Die Bücher der Könige (HKAT)*. Göttingen: Vandenhoeck & Ruprecht, 1900.

Kittel, Rudolf, and Kahle, Paul Ernst. *Biblia Hebraica*. 14th ed. Stuttgart: Württembergische Bibelanstalt, 1966.

Kitto, John. *A Cyclopaedia of Biblical Literature*. 2 vols. 1st ed. 1845; enlarged by William L. Alexander, 3 vols. Philadelphia: J. B. Lippincott Company, 3d ed. 1865.

Kleinert, Paul. *The Book of Obadiah, the Book of Jonah, the Book of Micah, the Book of Nahum, the Book of Habakkuk, the Book of Zephaniah (LCHS)*. New York: Charles Scribner's Sons, 1874.

Knight, George Angus Fulton. *Ruth and Jonah (TBC)*. London: SCM Press, Ltd., 1950.

_____. *Esther, Song of Songs, Lamentations (TBC)*. London: SCM Press, Ltd., 1955.

_____. *Deutero-Isaiah*. Nashville: Abingdon Press, 1965.

_____. *Hosea (TBC)*. London: SCM Press, Ltd., 1960.

Koch, Klaus. *The Rediscovery of Apocalyptic*. London: SCM Press, Ltd., 1972.

Koehler, Ludwig, and Baumgartner, Walter. *Lexicon in Veteris Testamenti Libros*. Leiden: E. J. Brill, 1958.

König, Eduard. *Das Deuteronomium (KAT)*. Leipzig: Deichert, 1917.

Kraus, Hans-Joachim. *Psalmen (BKAT)*. Neukirchen-Vluyn: Neukirchener Verlag, 1960.

_____. *Klagelieder (Threni) (BKAT)*. Neukirchen-Vluyn: Neukirchener Verlag, 1956.

Krouse, F. Michael. *Milton's Samson and the Christian Tradition*. Princeton: Princeton University Press, 1949.

Lambdin, Thomas O. *Introduction to Biblical Hebrew*. Charles Scribner's Sons, 1971.

Lamparter, Helmut. *Das Buch der Anfechtung (BAT)*. Stuttgart: Calwer Verlag, 1951.

————. *Das Buch der Sehnsucht. Das Buch Ruth. Das Hohe Lied. Die Klage-lieder (BAT)*. Stuttgart: Calwer Verlag, 1962.

————. *Das Buch der Psalmen (BAT)*. 2 vols. Stuttgart: Calwer Verlag, 1958; 2d ed. 1961.

————. *Das Buch der Weisheit (BAT)*. Stuttgart: Calwer Verlag, 2d ed. 1959.

————. *Prophet wider Willen (BAT)*. Stuttgart: Calwer Verlag, 1964.

————, and Ungern-Sternberg, Rolf Freiherr von. *Der Tag des Gerichtes Gottes. Die Propheten Habakuk, Zephanja, Jona, Nahum (BAT)*. Stuttgart: Calwer Verlag, 1960.

————. *Zum Wächter bestellt (BAT)*. Stuttgart: Calwer Verlag, 1968.

Lapide, Cornelius a. *Commentaria in Scripturam Sacram*. Antwerp: 1616. Often reprinted.

Lawson, George. *Lectures on the Book of Ruth*. 1805. Reprinted. Evansville, Ind.: Sovereign Grace Publishers, 1960.

Laymon, Charles M. (ed.). *The Interpreter's One-Volume Commentary on the Bible, Including the Apocrypha. With General Articles*. Nashville: Abingdon Press, 1971.

Leibowitz, Nehama. *Studies in the Book of Genesis*. Jerusalem: World Zionist Organization, 1972.

Le Long, Jacob. *Bibliotheca Sacra in binos syllabos distincta*. 2 vols. 3d ed. Paris, 1723.

Leslie, Elmer Archibald. *Jeremiah: Chronologically Arranged, Translated, and Interpreted*. Nashville: Abingdon Press, 1954.

Leupold, Herbert Carl. *Exposition of Genesis*. 2 vols. Grand Rapids: Baker Book House, 1942.

Lewis, Clive Staples. *Reflections on the Psalms*. New York: Harcourt, Brace and Company, Inc., 1958.

Lindsey, Hal. *The Late Great Planet Earth*. Grand Rapids: Zondervan Publishing House, 1970.

Lüthi, Walter. *Die Bauleute Gottes. Nehemia der Prophet im Kampf in den Aufbau der zerstörten Stadt*. Basel: Verlag F. Reinhardt, 1945.

————. *L'Ecclésiaste a vécu la vie*. Geneva: Éditions Labor et Fides, 1960.

Lumby, Joseph Rawson. *The First and Second Book of Kings (CB)*. Cambridge University Press, 1891.

Luther, Martin. *Complete Commentary on the First Twenty-two Psalms*. Tr. by H. Cole. 2 vols. London: W. Simpkin and R. Marshall, 1826.

————. *Luther's Works*. American Edition. St. Louis: Concordia Publishing House, 1955–.

Maier, Walter A. *The Book of Nahum*. St. Louis: Concordia Publishing House, 1959.

Mandelkern, Solomon. *Veteris Testamenti Concordantiae Hebraicae atque Chaldaicae*. 8th ed. Jerusalem: Schocken Books, Inc., 1969.

Martin, Hugh. *The Prophet Jonah*. 1866. Reprinted. London: Banner of Truth, 1958.

Mauchline, John. *I and II Samuel (NCeB)*. London: Oliphants, 1971.

———. *Isaiah 1–39 (TBC)*. London: SCM Press, Ltd., 1962.

Maurice, Frederick Denison. *The Prophets and Kings of the Old Testament*. London: Macmillan, 1904.

May, Herbert Gordon (ed.). *Oxford Bible Atlas*. 2d ed. London and New York: Oxford University Press, 1974.

Mays, James Luther. *The Book of Leviticus and the Book of Numbers (LaBC)*. Richmond: John Knox Press, 1963.

———. *Hosea (OTL)*. Philadelphia: The Westminster Press, 1969.

———. *Amos (OTL)*. Philadelphia: The Westminster Press, 1969.

———. *Micah (OTL)*. Philadelphia: The Westminster Press, 1976.

Maclaren, Alexander. *The Psalms (ExB)*. 3 vols. New York: Armstrong, 1891–1892.

McClintock, John, and Strong, James (eds.). *Cyclopedia of Biblical, Theological and Ecclesiastical Literature*. 12 vols. New York: Harper & Brothers, 1874–1887.

M'Caul, Alexander. *Rabbi David Kimchi's Commentary upon the Prophecies of Zechariah*. London: James Duncan, 1837.

McKane, William. *Proverbs (OTL)*. Philadelphia: The Westminster Press, 1970.

———. *I and II Samuel (TBC)*. London: SCM Press, Ltd., 1963.

McKenzie, John L. *The World of the Judges*. London: Geoffrey Chapman, Ltd., 1967.

———. *Second Isaiah. Introduction, Translation and Notes (AncB)*. New York: Doubleday & Company, Inc., 1968.

———. *A Theology of the Old Testament*. New York: Doubleday & Company, Inc., 1974.

McNeile, Alan Hugh. *The Book of Exodus (WC)*. London: Methuen & Co., Ltd., 1908.

———. *The Book of Numbers (CB)*. Cambridge University Press, 1911.

Meek, Theophile James. "The Song of Songs. Introduction and Exegesis," *The Interpreter's Bible*, Vol. V. Nashville: Abingdon Press, 1956. Pp. 91–98, 103–148.

Miller, J. Maxwell, and Tucker, Gene M. *The Book of Joshua (CNEB)*. Cambridge University Press, 1974.

Miller, Madeleine Sweeny, and Miller, John Lane. *Harper's Bible Dictionary*. 8th ed. New York: Harper & Brothers, 1973.

Mitchell, Hinckley Gilbert Thomas; Smith, J. M. Powis; Bewer, Julius A. *A Critical and Exegetical Commentary on Haggai, Zechariah, Malachi, and Jonah (ICC)*. Edinburgh: T. & T. Clark, 1912.

Montgomery, James Alan. *A Critical and Exegetical Commentary on the Books of Kings (ICC)*. Edinburgh: T. & T. Clark, 1951.

_____. *A Critical and Exegetical Commentary on the Book of Daniel (ICC)*. Edinburgh: T. & T. Clark, 1927.

Moore, Carey A. *Esther (AncB)*. New York: Doubleday & Company, Inc., 1971.

Moore, George Foot. *A Critical and Exegetical Commentary on Judges (ICC)*. Edinburgh: T. & T. Clark, 1895.

Moore, Thomas Verner. *A Commentary on Zechariah*. 1856. Reprinted. London: Banner of Truth, 1958.

Morgan, George Campbell. *Studies in the Prophecy of Jeremiah*. London: Oliphants, 1963.

Mowinckel, Sigmund. *The Psalms in Israel's Worship*. 2 vols. Oxford: Basil Blackwell, 1962.

_____. *Zur Komposition des Buches Jeremia*. Kristiania: J. Dybwad, 1914.

Muilenburg, James. "The Book of Isaiah, Chs. 40–66. Introduction and Exegesis," *The Interpreter's Bible*, Vol. V. Nashville: Abingdon Press, 1956. Pp. 381–773.

Myers, Jacob Martin. "The Book of Judges. Introduction and Exegesis," *The Interpreter's Bible*, Vol. II. Nashville: Abingdon Press, 1953. Pp. 677–826.

_____. *I and II Chronicles (AncB)*. New York: Doubleday & Company, Inc., 1965.

_____. *Ezra, Nehemiah (AncB)*. Doubleday & Company, Inc., 1965.

Neale, John Mason, and Littledale, Richard F. *A Commentary on the Psalms from Primitive and Mediaeval Writers*. 4 vols. London: J. Masten and Co., 1860; 4th ed. 1884.

Neubauer, Adolphe, and Driver, Samuel Rolles. *The Fifty-third Chapter of Isaiah According to the Jewish Interpreters*. 2 vols. 1876. Reprinted. New York: Ktav Publishing House, Inc., 1970.

Nicholson, Ernest W. *Deuteronomy and Tradition*. Oxford: Basil Blackwell, 1967.

_____. *Jeremiah 1–26; Jeremiah 27–52 (CNEB)*. 2 vols. Cambridge University Press, 1973–1975.

North, Christopher Richard. *The Second Isaiah: Introduction, Translation and Commentary to Chs. XL–LV*. Oxford: Clarendon Press, 1964.

_____. *The Suffering Servant in Deutero-Isaiah: Historical and Critical Studies*. 2d ed. London: Oxford University Press, 1956.

Noth, Martin. *Exodus (OTL)*. Philadelphia: The Westminster Press, 1962.

_____. *Leviticus (OTL)*. Philadelphia: The Westminster Press, 1965.

_____. *Numbers (OTL)*. Philadelphia: The Westminster Press, 1969.

_____. *Das Buch Josua (HAT)*. 2d ed. Tübingen: J. C. B. Mohr, 1953.

_____. *The History of Israel*. New York: Harper & Brothers, 1958; rev. ed. 1960.

————. *Könige (BKAT)*. Neukirchen-Vluyn: Neukirchener Verlag, 1968.

Oehler, Gustav Friedrich. *Theology of the Old Testament*. 2 vols. Edinburgh: T. & T. Clark, 1874.

Oesterley, William Oscar Emil. *The Psalms*. London: S.P.C.K., 1939.

————. *The Book of Proverbs (WC)*. London: Methuen & Co., Ltd., 1929.

Origen. *The Song of Songs. Commentary and Homilies (Ancient Christian Writers)*. Westminster, Md.: The Newman Press, 1957.

Orme, William. *Bibliotheca Biblica: A Select List of Books on Sacred Literature*. Edinburgh: Adam Black, 1824.

Orr, James (ed.). *The International Standard Bible Encyclopaedia*. 5 vols. Rev. ed. Chicago: Howard Severance, 1930.

Parker, Thomas Henry Louis. *Calvin's New Testament Commentaries*. London: SCM Press, Ltd., 1971.

Paton, Lewis Bayles. *A Critical and Exegetical Commentary on the Book of Esther (ICC)*. Edinburgh: T. & T. Clark, 1908.

Peake, Arthur Samuel. *Job (CeB)*. Edinburgh: T . C. & C. E. Jack, 1904.

————. *Jeremiah and Lamentations (CeB)*. 2 vols. Edinburgh: T. C. & C. E. Jack, 1910–1911.

————(ed.). *A Commentary on the Bible*. London: Nelson, [ca. 1920].

Pearson, John, *et al. Critici Sacri sive doctissimorum vivorum in S. S. Biblia Annotationes et Tractatus*. 13 vols. Folio. Amsterdam, 1698–1732.

Perlitt, Lothar. *Bundestheologie im Alten Testament*. Neukirchen-Vluyn: Neukirchener Verlag, 1969.

Perowne, John James Stewart. *The Book of Psalms*. 2 vols. London: George Bell and Sons, 1st ed. 1864–1868; 7th ed. 1890.

Perowne, Thomas Thomason. *Jonah (CB)*. Cambridge University Press, 1880.

Phillips, Anthony. *Deuteronomy (CNEB)*. Cambridge University Press, 1973.

Plastaras, James. *The God of Exodus: The Theology of the Exodus Narratives*. Milwaukee: Bruce Publishing Co., 1966.

Plöger, Otto. *Das Buch Daniel (KAT)*. Gütersloh: Gütersloher Verlagshaus Gerd Mohn, 1965.

Plumptre, Edward Hayes. *Ecclesiastes (CB)*. Cambridge University Press, 1881.

Podechard, Edouard. *L'Ecclésiaste (ETB)*. Paris: J. Gabalda, 1912.

Poole, Matthew. *Synopsis Criticorum aliorumque Sacrae Scripturae Interpretum et commentatorum*. 5 vols. Folio. London, 1669–1676.

Pope, Marvin H. *Job (AncB)*. New York: Doubleday & Company, Inc., 1st ed. 1965; rev. ed. 1973.

Porteous, Norman W. *Daniel (OTL)*. Philadelphia: The Westminster Press, 1965.

Preus, James Samuel. *From Shadow to Promise. Old Testament from Augustine to the Younger Luther.* Cambridge, Mass.: Harvard University Press, 1964.

Pusey, Edward Bouverie. *The Minor Prophets.* 2 vols. New York: Funk and Wagnalls, 1885.

Rad, Gerhard von. *Genesis (OTL).* Philadelphia: The Westminster Press, 1st ed. 1961; rev. ed. 1973.

————. *Deuteronomy (OTL).* Philadelphia: The Westminster Press, 1966.

————. *Studies in Deuteronomy.* London: SCM Press, Ltd., 1953.

————. "The Levitical Sermon in I and II Chronicles," *The Problem of the Hexateuch and Other Essays.* New York: McGraw-Hill Book Co., Inc., 1966. Pp. 267ff.

————. *Predigten.* Munich: Chr. Kaiser Verlag, 1972.

————. *Wisdom in Israel.* Nashville: Abingdon Press, 1972.

————. *Old Testament Theology.* 2 vols. New York: Harper & Row, Publishers, Inc., 1962.

————Rahlfs, Alfred. *Septuaginta, id est, Vetus Testamentum Graece iuxta LXX interpretes.* 2 vols. 8th ed. Stuttgart: Württembergische Bibelanstalt, 1965.

Redpath, Henry Adeney. *The Book of the Prophet Ezekiel (WC).* London: Methuen & Co., Ltd., 1907.

Richardson, Alan. *Genesis I-XI (TBC).* London: SCM Press, Ltd., 1953.

————(ed.). *A Theological Word Book of the Bible.* London: SCM Press, Ltd., 1950.

Ringgren, Helmer. *The Faith of the Psalmists.* Philadelphia: Fortress Press, 1963.

————, and Weiser, Artur. *Das Hohe Lied. Klagelieder. Das Buch Esther (ATD).* Göttingen: Vandenhoeck & Ruprecht, 1958.

————, and Zimmerli, Walther. *Sprüche, Prediger (ATD).* Göttingen: Vandenhoeck & Ruprecht, 1962.

Robert, André; Tournay, René; and Feuillet, André. *Le Cantique des Cantiques (ETB).* Paris: J. Gabalda, 1963.

Robertson, Frederick William. *Notes on Genesis.* London: Henry S. King, 1877.

Robinson, George Livingstone. *The Twelve Minor Prophets.* New York: Harper & Brothers, 1926. Reprinted. Grand Rapids: Baker Book House, 1972.

Robinson, Henry Wheeler. *The Cross in the Old Testament.* London: SCM Press, Ltd., 1955.

————. *Two Hebrew Prophets: Studies in Hosea and Ezekiel.* London: Lutterworth Press, 1948.

Robinson, Joseph. *The First Book of Kings (CNEB).* Cambridge University Press, 1972.

Robinson, Theodore Henry, and Horst, Friedrich. *Die zwölf Kleinen Propheten (HAT)*. Tübingen: J. C. B. Mohr, 1st ed. 1938; 3d ed. 1964.

Rosenmüller, Ernst Friedrich Karl. *Scholia in Vetus Testamentum*. 25 vols. Leipzig: J. A. Barth, 1788–1835.

Rothstein, Johann Wilhelm, and Hänel, Johannes. *Kommentar zum ersten Buch der Chronik (KAT)*. Leipzig: Deichert, 1927.

Rowley, Harold Henry. "The Marriage of Ruth," *The Servant of the Lord and Other Essays on the Old Testament*. London: Lutterworth Press, 1952. Pp. 163–186.

————. *Job (NCeB)*. London: Thomas Nelson & Sons, 1970.

————. "The Interpretation of the Song of Songs," *The Servant of the Lord and Other Essays on the Old Testament*. London: Lutterworth Press, 1952. Pp. 197ff.

————. *The Revelance of Apocalyptic*. Rev. ed. New York: Harper & Brothers, 1955.

————(ed.). *Eleven Years of Bible Bibliography*. Indian Hills, Colo.: The Falcon's Wing Press, 1957.

Rudolph, Wilhelm. *Das Buch Ruth. Das Hohe Lied. Die Klagelieder (KAT)*. Gütersloh: Gütersloher Verlagshaus Gerd Mohn, 1962.

————, *Chronikbücher (HAT)*. Tübingen: J. C. B. Mohr, 1955.

————.*Esra und Nehemia (HAT)*. Tübingen: J. C. B. Mohr, 1949.

————. *Jeremia (HAT)*. 3d ed. Tübingen: J. C. B. Mohr, 1968.

————. *Hosea (KAT)*. Gütersloh: Gütersloher Verlagshaus Gerd Mohn, 1966.

————. *Joel, Amos, Obadja, Jona (KAT)*. Gütersloh: Gütersloher Verlagshaus Gerd Mohn, 1971.

————. *Micha, Nahum, Habakuk, Zephanja (KAT)*. Gütersloh: Gütersloher Verlagshaus Gerd Mohn, 1975.

Ryle, Herbert Edward. *The Books of Ezra and Nehemiah (CB)*. Cambridge University Press, 1917.

Šanda, Albert. *Die Bücher der Könige (ExHAT)*. 2 vols. Münster: Aschendorf, 1911.

Sarna, Nahum M. *Understanding Genesis*. New York: McGraw-Hill Book Co., Inc., 1966.

Schaff, Philip (ed.). *The Minor Prophets (LCHS)*. New York: Charles Scribner's, 1874.

Schildenberger, Johannes B., and Miller, Athanasius. *Die Bücher Tobias, Judith und Esther (HSAT)*. Bonn: Hanstein, 1940–1941.

Schmidt, Hans. *Die Psalmen (HAT)*. Tübingen: J. C. B. Mohr, 1934.

Schmidt, Werner H. *Exodus (BKAT)*. Neukirchen-Vluyn: Neukirchener Verlag, 1974–.

Schultz, Hermann. *Old Testament Theology*. 2 vols. 2d ed. Edinburgh: T. & T. Clark, 1895.

Scott, Robert Balgarnie Young. *Proverbs and Ecclesiastes (AncB).* New York: Doubleday & Company, Inc., 1965.

————."The Book of Isaiah, Chs. 1–39. Introduction and Exegesis," *The Interpreter's Bible,* Vol. V. Nashville: Abingdon Press, 1956. Pp. 151–381.

Scott, Thomas. *The Holy Bible, containing the Old and New Testaments, according to the Authorised Version, with Explanatory Notes.* London: L. B. Seeley and Son, 1827.

Sellin, Ernst. *Das Zwölfprophetenbuch (KAT).* 2 vols. 2d and 3d eds. Leipzig: Deichert, 1929–1930.

The Septuagint Version of the Old Testament with an English Translation. London: S. Bagster & Sons, n.d.

Simon, Ulrich Ernst. *A Theology of Salvation: A Commentary on Isaiah 40–55.* London: S.P.C.K., 1953.

Skinner, John. *A Critical and Exegetical Commentary on the Book of Genesis (ICC).* Edinburgh: T. & T. Clark, 1st ed. 1910; 2d ed. 1930.

————. *Kings (CeB).* Edinburgh: T. C. & E. C. Jack, 1904.

————. *Isaiah (CB).* 2 vols. Cambridge University Press, 1910,1915.

————. *Prophecy and Religion.* Cambridge University Press, 1922.

Smalley, Beryl. *The Study of the Bible in the Middle Ages.* Oxford: Basil Blackwell, 2d ed. 1952. Reprinted. Notre Dame Press, 1964.

Smart, James Dick. *History and Theology in Second Isaiah.* Philadelphia: The Westminster Press, 1965.

Smith, George Adam. *The Book of Deuteronomy (CB).* Cambridge University Press, 1918.

————. *The Book of Isaiah (ExB).* 2 vols. New York: Armstrong, 1888. Rev ed. New York: Harper & Brothers, 1927.

————.*Jeremiah.* New York: Doran, 1923. 4th ed. New York: Doubleday & Company, Inc., 1929.

————. *The Book of the Twelve Prophets (ExB).* 2 vols. New York: Armstrong, 1908. Rev. ed. New York: Harper & Brothers, 1928.

————. *The Historical Geography of the Holy Land.* London: Hodder & Stoughton, 1st ed. 1894; 11th ed. 1904.

Smith, Henry Preserved. *A Critical and Exegetical Commentary on the Books of Samuel (ICC).* Edinburgh: T. & T. Clark, 1904.

Smith, John Merlin Powis; Ward, William Hayes; Bewer, Julius A. *A Critical and Exegetical Commentary on Micah, Zephaniah, Nahum, Habakkuk, Obadiah, and Joel (ICC).* Edinburgh: T. & T. Clark, 1911.

Smith, Wilbur Moorehead. *Profitable Bible Study.* Boston: W. A. Wilde Co., 1939. 2d rev. ed. Grand Rapids: Baker Book House, 1963.

Smith, William (ed.), *Dictionary of the Bible.* Rev. by Horatio Balch Hackett and Ezra Abbot. 4 vols. Boston: Houghton, Mifflin and Co., 1885.

Snaith, Norman Henry. *Leviticus, Numbers (NCeB)*. London: Thomas Nelson & Sons, 1967.

———. *The Book of Job. Its Origin and Purpose*. London: SCM Press, Ltd., 1969.

———(ed.). *Sepher Torah, Nebi'im U-Kethubim*. London: The British and Foreign Bible Society, 1958.

Soggin, Juan Alberto. *Joshua (OTL)*. Philadelphia: The Westminster Press, 1972.

Speiser, Ephraim Avigdon. *Genesis (AncB)*. New York: Doubleday & Company, Inc., 1964.

Spurgeon, Charles Haddon. *Commenting and Commentaries*. London: Passmore and Alabaster, 1876.

———. *The Treasury of David*. 7 vols. London: London: Passmore and Alabaster, 1870–1885.

Spurrell, George James. *Notes on the Hebrew Text of the Book of Genesis*. London: Frowde, 1st ed. 1887; 2d ed. 1896.

Stamm, Johann Jakob, and Andrew, Maurice Edward. *The Ten Commandments in Recent Research*. London: SCM Press, Ltd., 1967.

Steuernagel, Carl. *Das Deuteronomium (HKAT)*. 2d ed. Göttingen: Vandenhoeck & Ruprecht, 1923.

Stoebe, Hans Joachim. *Das erste Buch Samuelis (KAT)*. Gütersloh: Gütersloher Verlagshaus Gerd Mohn, 1973.

Strahan, James. *The Book of Job*. 2d ed. Edinburgh: T. & T. Clark, 1914.

Streane, Annesley William. *The Book of Esther (CB)*. Cambridge University Press, 1907.

———. *Jeremiah and Lamentations (CB)*. Cambridge University Press, 1899.

Strong, James. *The Exhaustive Concordance of the Bible*. Nashville: Abingdon, 1890.

———. *The Student's Commentary on the Book of Ecclesiastes*. New York: Hunt and Easton, 1893.

Stuart, Alexander Moody. *Exposition in Song of Solomon*. London: Nisbet, 1860.

Swete, Henry Barclay (ed.). *The Old Testament in Greek According to the Septuagint*. 3 vols. Cambridge University Press, 1895–1899.

Terrien, Samuel. "The Book of Job. Introduction and Exegesis," *The Interpreter's Bible*, Vol. III. Nashville: Abingdon Press, 1954. Pp. 877–905, 908–1198.

———. *Job: Poet of Existence*. Indianapolis: The Bobbs-Merrill Company, Inc., 1957.

Thiele, Edwin Richard. *The Mysterious Numbers of the Hebrew Kings*. Rev. ed. Grand Rapids: Wm. B. Eerdmans, 1965.

Thielicke, Helmut. *How the World Began*. Philadelphia: Muhlenberg Press, 1961.

Thomas, David Winton (ed.). *Archaeology and Old Testament Study*. Oxford: Clarendon Press, 1967.

Thompson, John A. *Deuteronomy: An Introduction and Commentary (TOTC)*. London: Inter-Varsity Press, 1974.

Torrey, Charles Cutler. *The Second Isaiah: A New Interpretation*. New York: Charles Scribner's Sons, 1928.

Toy, Crawford Howell. *A Critical and Exegetical Commentary on the Book of Proverbs (ICC)*. Edinburgh: T. & T. Clark, 1904.

Tucker, Gene M. (ed.). *Guides to Biblical Scholarship*. Philadelphia: Fortress Press, 1971–.

Unger, Merrill Frederick. *Introductory Guide to the Old Testament*. Grand Rapids: Zondervan Publishing House, 1951.

———. *Zechariah: Prophet of Messiah's Glory*. Grand Rapids: Zondervan Publishing House, 1963.

Ungern-Sternberg, Rolf Freiherr von, and Lamparter, Helmut. *Der Tag des Gerichtes Gottes. Die Propheten Habakuk, Zephanja, Jona, Nahum (BAT)*. Stuttgart: Calwer Verlag, 1960.

Vaux, Roland de. *Ancient Israel*. New York: McGraw-Hill Book Co., Inc., 1961.

Vischer, Wilhelm. *Esther (Theologische Existenz Heute, 48)*. Munich: Chr. Kaiser Verlag, 1937.

———. *Hiob. Ein Zeuge Jesu Christi*. 6th ed. Zurich: Evangelischer Verlag, 1947.

———. *Der Prediger Salomo*. Munich: Chr. Kaiser Verlag, 1926.

———. *The Witness of the Old Testament to Christ*. Vol. I. London: Lutterworth Press, 1949.

Volz, Paul. *Jesaia II (KAT)*. Leipzig: Deichert, 1932.

———. *Der Prophet Jeremia (KAT)*. 2d ed. Leipzig: Deichert, 1928.

Vriezen, Theodorus Christian. *An Outline of Old Testament Theology*. Boston: Charles T. Branford, 1958.

Wade, George Woosung. *The Books of the Prophets. Micah, Obadiah, Joel, and Jonah (WC)*. London: Methuen & Co., Ltd., 1925.

Walch, Johann Georg. *Bibliotheca Theologica Selecta, literaliis adnotationibus instructa*. Vol. IV. Jena: Sumtu Viduae Croeckerianae, 1765.

Walvoord, John Flipse. *Daniel. The Key to Prophetic Revelation*. Chicago: Moody Press, 1971.

Ward, James M. *Hosea: A Theological Commentary*. New York: Harper & Row, Publishers, Inc., 1966.

Watson, Robert Alexander. *Judges and Ruth (ExB)*. New York: Armstrong, 1889.

Watts, Isaac. *The Psalms, Hymns and Spiritual Songs of the Rev. Isaac Watts.* Ed. by Samuel Worchester. Boston: Crocker & Brewster, 1841.

Watts, John D. W. *Vision and Prophecy in Amos.* Leiden: E. J. Brill, 1958.

_____. *Obadiah: A Critical, Exegetical Commentary.* Grand Rapids: Wm. B. Eerdmans Publishing Company, 1969.

Weinfeld, Moshe. *Deuteronomy and the Deuteronomic School.* Oxford: Clarendon Press, 1972.

Weiser, Artur. *Das Buch Hiob (ATD).* 5th ed. Göttingen: Vandenhoeck & Ruprecht, 1968.

_____. *The Psalms (OTL).* Philadelphia: The Westminster Press, 1962.

_____, and Ringgren, Helmer. *Das Hohe Lied. Klagelieder. Das Buch Esther (ATD).* Göttingen: Vandenhoeck & Ruprecht, 1958.

_____. *Das Buch des Propheten Jeremia (ATD).* 6th ed. Göttingen: Vandenhoeck & Ruprecht, 1952, 1969.

_____, and Elliger, Karl. *Das Buch der zwölf Kleinen Propheten (ATD).* 2 vols. Göttingen: Vandenhoeck & Ruprecht, 1949,1950.

Welch, Adam Cleghorn. *The Code of Deuteronomy.* London: James Clarke, 1924.

_____. *Deuteronomy: The Framework to the Code.* London: Oxford University Press, 1932.

_____. *Kings and Prophets of Israel.* London: Lutterworth Press, 1952.

_____. *Jeremiah, His Time and His Work.* Oxford: Basil Blackwell, 1951.

_____. *Visions of the End. A Study in Daniel and Revelation.* London: James Clarke, 1922.

Westermann, Claus. *Genesis 1–11 (BKAT).* Neukirchen-Vluyn: Neukirchener Verlag, 1974.

_____. *Isaiah 40–66 (OTL).* Philadelphia: The Westminster Press, 1969.

Wevers, John William. *Ezekiel (NCeB).* London: Thomas Nelson & Sons, 1969.

Whybray, Roger Norman. *The Book of Proverbs (CNEB).* Cambridge University Press, 1972.

_____. *Isaiah 40–66 (NCeB).* London: Oliphants, 1975.

Wildberger, Hans. *Jesaja I (1–12) (BKAT).* Neukirchen-Vluyn: Neukirchener Verlag, 1972

Williams, Arnold. *The Common Expositor.* Chapel Hill: University of North Carolina Press, 1948.

Williams, Arthur Lukyn. *Ecclesiastes (CB).* Rev. ed. Cambridge University Press, 1922.

Winer, Georg Benedict. *Handbuch der theologischen Literatur.* 2 vols. 3d ed. Leipzig: C. H. Reclam, 1838–1840.

Wolf, Hans Heinrich. *Die Einheit des Bundes. Das Verhältnis von Altem und Neuem Testament bei Calvin.* Neukirchen: Verlag der Buchhandlung des Erziehungsverein, 1958.

Wolff, Hans Walter. *Hosea (Her)*. Philadelphia: Fortress Press, 1974.
_____. *Amos and Joel (Her)*. Philadelphia: Fortress Press, 1977.
_____. *Studien zum Jonabuch*. Neukirchen-Vluyn: Neukirchener Verlag, 1965.
Woude, Adam Simon van der. *Micha (POT)*. Nijkerk: G. F. Callenbach, 1976.
Wright, Charles Henry Hamilton. *Zechariah and His Prophecies*. London: Hodder & Stoughton, 1879.
Wright, George Ernest. *Biblical Archaeology*. Rev. ed. Philadelphia: The Westminster Press, 1962.
_____. "The Book of Deuteronomy. Introduction and Exegesis," *The Interpreter's Bible*, Vol. II. Nashville: Abingdon Press, 1953. Pp. 309–537.
_____. *The Book of Isaiah (LaBC)*. Richmond: John Knox Press, 1964.
Wright, George Ernest, and Filson, Floyd V. *The Westminster Historical Atlas to the Bible*. Rev. ed. Philadelphia: The Westminster Press, 1956.
Würthwein, Ernst. *Die fünf Megilloth (HAT)*. 2d ed. Tübingen: J. C. B. Mohr, 1969.
Young, Edward Joseph. *An Introduction to the Old Testament*. Rev. ed. Grand Rapids: Wm. B. Eerdmans Publishing Company, 1960.
_____. *The Book of Isaiah*. 3 vols. Grand Rapids: Wm. B. Eerdmans Publishing Company, 1965–1972.
_____. *The Prophecy of Daniel: A Commentary*. Grand Rapids: Wm. B. Eerdmans Publishing Company, 1949.
Young, Robert. *Analytical Concordance to the Bible*. New York: Funk & Wagnalls, n.d.
Zimmerli, Walther. *I. Mose 1–11. Die Urgeschichte (ZB)*. Zurich: Zwingli Verlag, 1st ed. 1943; 3d ed. 1967.
_____. *Prediger (ATD)*. Göttingen: Vandenhoeck & Ruprecht, 1962.
_____. *Ezekiel (BKAT)*. 2 vols. Neukirchen-Vluyn: Neukirchener Verlag, 1969.
_____. *The Law and the Prophets*. Oxford: Basil Blackwell, 1965.
Zöckler, Otto. *The Book of Chronicles (LCHS)*. New York: Charles Scribner's, 1879.
_____. *The Song of Solomon (LCHS)*. New York: Charles Scribner's, 1873.
_____. *Daniel (LCHS)*. New York: Charles Scribner's, 1871.
Zuchold, Ernst Amandus. *Bibliotheca Theologica*. 2 vols. Göttingen: Vandenhoeck & Ruprecht, 1864.

Appendix

A Selection of Secondhand Bookstores in Theology

A complete listing of secondhand book dealers is published every two years by the Sheppard Press, London, under the titles: *Book Dealers in North America, European Bookdealers,* and *A Directory of Dealers in Secondhand and Antiquarian Books in the British Isles.* I also recommend a fascinating new book by Roy H. Lewis entitled *The Book Browser's Guide: Britain's Secondhand and Antiquarian Bookshops* (London: David and Charles, 1975).

The following are among the most active dealers :

1. *The United States*

   Alec R. Allenson, Box 31, Naperville, Ill. 60540
   Baker Book House, 1019 Wealthy St., S.E., Grand Rapids, Mich. 49506
   Kregel's Bookstore, 525 Eastern Ave., Grand Rapids, Mich. 49503
   Noah's Ark Book Attic, Stony Point, Rt.2, Greenwood, S.C. 29646

2. *Great Britain*

   B. H. Blackwell, Ltd., 50 Broad Street, Oxford, England OX1 3BQ
   Holleyman and Son, 59 Carlisle Road, Hove, Sussex, England BN3 4FQ
   Howes Bookshop, 3 Trinity St., Hastings, Sussex, England TN34 1HQ
   James Thin, 53–59 South Bridge, Edinburgh, Scotland

3. *Netherlands for all European books*

   Antiquariaat Spinoza, Den Texstraat 26, Amsterdam, Netherlands
   T. Wever, Boekhandel, Franeker, Netherlands

   B. H. Blackwell's catalogues on Biblica, Patristica, and Theology are invaluable guides to all new books in the field.

Index

Ackroyd, P. R., 13, 49, 53, 54
Adar, Z., 47
Albright, W. F., 24, 45
Anderson, A. A., 61
Anderson, B. W., 22, 56
Augustine, Saint, 29, 62f., 64

Baehr, K. C. W. F., 52
Baentsch, B., 39, 41, 42
Baker, R., 63
Baldwin, J. G., 87
Bardtke, H., 56
Barnes, W. E., 51, 62
Barr, J., 26, 33
Barth, K., 37, 40, 52, 59, 68, 74
Barton, G. A., 67
Barucq, A., 65
Batten, L. W., 54
Bentzen, A., 80
Bertheau, E., 53, 55
Bevan, A. A., 79
Bickerman, E., 86
Binns, L. E., 42, 75
Blaikie, W. G., 46, 50
Boling, R. G., 47
Bonar, A. A., 41–42
Bonhoeffer, D., 37, 64
Braude, W. G., 64
Brenz, J., 29, 67
Bridges, C., 65
Briggs, C. A., 16, 60
Bright, J., 24, 45, 74f.
Brockington, L. H., 54
Brown, S. L., 84

Brunner, R., 79
Buber, M., 40, 47
Budde, K., 49, 69
Buis, P., 43
Burney, C. F., 46, 51
Burrowes, G., 68
Buttrick, G. A., 19
Buzy, D., 70

Calmet, A., 14, 30
Calvin, J., 29, 36, 40, 42, 44,
    46, 50, 59, 62, 63, 72, 74,
    81, 88
Campbell, E. F., Jr., 48
Cassuto, U., 37, 38
Charles, R. H., 80
Cheyne, T. K., 20, 72
Childs, B. S., 38
Clarke, A., 30
Clements, R. E., 39, 44
Cole, R. A., 39
Cooke, G. A., 46, 47, 48, 77
Cornill, C. H., 75
Cox, S., 58
Craigie, P. C., 43
Cripps, R. S., 85
Cunliffe-Jones, H., 43
Curtis, E. L., 53

Dahood, M., 60f.
Danker, F. W., 13, 15, 19, 31
Davidson, A. B., 27, 50, 58, 78,
    86
Davidson, R., 37

Davies, G. H., 39
Deissler, A., 62
Delcor, M., 79
Delitzsch, F., 32, 36f., 58, 61, 65,
  67, 68, 69, 71, 82
Dhorme, E., 57
Dickson, D., 63
Dillmann, A., 37, 43
Dods, M., 38
Driver, S. R., 16, 36, 38f., 43, 49,
  57, 74, 80, 85, 87
Duhm, B., 72, 75

Eaton, J. H., 87
Eichrodt, W., 26, 38, 73, 78
Elliger, K., 41, 83
Ellul, J., 52, 86
Elmslie, W. A. L., 53

Fairbairn, P., 78, 86
Farrar, F. W., 52, 80
Feinberg, C. L., 79
Feuillet, A., 70
Fichtner, J., 51, 52
Fohrer, G., 22, 57, 78
Fricke, K. D., 52

Galling, K., 30, 54, 67, 87
Garstang, J., 45f.
Gehman, H. S., 19
Gemser, B., 65
Gerleman, G., 48, 56, 69
Gibson, E. C. S., 58
Gill, J., 68
Ginsburg, C. D., 66
Glanzman, G. S., 13
Goettsberger, J., 54, 81
Gordis, R., 66, 69
Gottwald, N. K., 22, 76
Gray, G. B., 42, 57, 72
Gray, J., 45, 47, 50f.
Gregory the Great, 29, 59
Gressmann, H., 39, 49
Gros Louis, K. R. R., 47, 48

Gunkel, H., 35, 36, 39, 56, 60,
  62, 63, 77
Gutbrod, K., 50

Haller, M., 56, 77
Harper, A., 70
Harper, W. R., 82, 85
Harrison, R. K., 22, 75
Hastings, J., 20
Heaton, E. W., 80
Hengstenberg, E. W., 62, 67, 78
Henry, M., 30
Herbert, A. S., 37, 73
Herrmann, J., 78
Hertzberg, H. W., 45, 47, 48, 49,
  67
Hillers, D. R., 76
Hippolytus, 81
Hölscher, G., 57
Hoffmann, D., 41
Hoonacker, A. van, 83
Horst, F., 83
Hyatt, J. P., 39, 75, 76

Jacob, B., 37
Jacob, E., 26, 83
Jeffery, A., 80
Jerome, Saint, 29, 63, 74, 81,
  86
Jones, D. R., 85, 87
Joüon, P., 48
Jung, C., 59

Keil, C. F., 32, 37, 46, 47, 52, 53,
  55, 56, 78, 80, 82
Keller, C. A., 83
Kennedy, A. R. S., 41, 42, 49
Kidner, D., 36, 37, 40, 65
Kimhi, D., 64
Kirkpatrick, A. F., 49, 61
Kissane, E. J., 61, 72
Kittel, G., 20f.
Kittel, R., 15
Kleinert, P., 82

118

Knight, G. A. F., 48, 56, 69, 73, 74, 77
Kraus, H.-J., 62, 76
Krouse, F. M., 48

Lamparter, H., 48, 58, 62, 65, 69f., 75, 77, 79, 87
Leupold, H. C., 36
Lüthi, W., 55, 68, 81
Lumby, J. R., 51
Luther, M., 18, 29, 36, 40, 44, 62, 63, 88

Maier, W. A., 87
Mauchline, J., 49, 73
Maurice, F. D., 52
May, H. G., 24, 78
Mays, J. L., 41, 42, 84, 85, 86
Maclaren, A., 64
McKane, W., 49, 65
McKenzie, J. L., 26, 47, 73
McNeile, A. H., 39, 42
Meek, T. J., 17, 69
Miller, J. M., 46
Montgomery, J. A., 50, 51, 79
Moore, C. A., 56
Moore, G. F., 46
Morgan, G. C., 76
Mowinckel, S., 60
Muilenburg, J., 73
Murphy, R. E., 66
Myers, J. M., 53, 54

Nicholson, E. W., 44, 64, 75
North, C. R., 73, 74
Noth, M., 24, 39, 41, 42, 45, 51

Oesterley, W. O. E., 62, 65
Origen, 29

Paton, L. B., 55f.
Peake, A. S., 33, 34, 58, 75, 77
Perowne, J. J. S., 61
Phillips, A., 43

Plastaras, J., 40
Plöger, O., 76, 77, 80
Plumptre, E. H., 67
Podechard, E., 67
Poole, M., 29
Pope, M. H., 57
Porteous, N. W., 80
Pusey, E. B., 82

Rad, G. von, 26, 35, 38, 42, 43f., 49, 54, 64, 84
Redpath, H. A., 78
Richardson, A., 21, 37
Ringgren, H., 21, 56, 60, 69
Robert, A., 62, 70
Robertson, F. W., 38
Robinson, G. L., 88
Robinson, H. W., 59, 76, 84
Robinson, J., 51
Robinson, T. H., 83
Rosenmüller, E. F. K., 30
Rothstein, J. W., 53f.
Rowley, H. H., 13, 33, 48, 58, 81
Rudolph, W., 48, 53, 54, 69, 75, 76, 77, 83, 84, 85, 86
Ryle, H. E., 55

Šanda, A., 51
Sarna, N. M., 36
Schildenberger, J. B., 56
Schmidt, W. H., 39
Scott, R. B. Y., 33, 64f., 66, 72
Scott, T., 30, 72
Sellin, E., 83
Simon, U. E., 73
Skinner, J., 36, 51, 71, 76
Smart, J. D., 73f.
Smith, G. A., 24, 43, 71, 75, 82
Smith, H. P., 49
Snaith, N. H., 15, 41, 42
Soggin, J. A., 45
Speiser, E. A., 36
Spurgeon, C. H., 14, 63

Stamm, J. J., 40
Stoebe, H. J., 49f.
Strahan, J., 58
Streane, A. W., 41, 56, 77
Strong, J., 16, 20, 66
Stuart, A. M., 68

Terrien, S., 58
Thiele, E. R., 52
Thielicke, H., 38
Thompson, J. A., 43
Torrey, C. C., 73
Toy, C. H., 65
Tucker, G. M., 22f., 46

Unger, M. F., 22, 87
Ungern-Sternberg, R. von, 87

Vischer, W., 38, 56, 68
Volz, P., 75

Walvoord, J. F., 80
Ward, J. M., 84
Watson, R. A., 47
Watts, J. D. W., 85, 86
Weiser, A., 58, 61, 75, 77, 83
Welch, A. C., 44, 50, 76, 81
Westermann, C., 37, 73
Wevers, J. W., 78
Whybray, R. N., 65, 73
Wildberger, H., 73
Williams, A. L., 66
Wolff, H. W., 83, 84, 85, 86
Woude, A. S. van der, 86
Wright, G. E., 24, 43, 72
Würthwein, E., 48, 56, 69

Young, E. J., 22, 72, 80

Zimmerli, W., 37, 40, 67, 77, 78
Zöckler, O., 53, 69, 80